The Case For Tribulation Saints and the Post-Tribulation Rapture of the Church

By: Shawn M Teats

The Case for Tribulation Saints and the Post-Tribulation Rapture of the Church by Shawn M. Teats

All scripture references in this book are from the King James Version of the Bible unless otherwise noted.

Printed in the United States of America
First Publication, 2015

ISBN

Publishing and Distribution Services: bookbaby.com

Cover Design Services: myecovermaker.com

Christian Crown Publisher
14 Crown Street
Stafford Springs, CT 06076

Table of Contents

Acknowledgements

I give thanks to my Lord Jesus Christ for the consistent nudging to write this book and for opening the scriptures to understanding.

I thank my wife, Jennifer, for her encouragement and support in the writing of this book and for standing by my side in ministry.

I thank my children, Jacob, Caleb, and Kylee for their support and for the time spent away from them in study, prayer, and ministry.

I thank Brother Irvin Baxter of Endtime Ministries for his unfeigned faith in the Lord. Our meeting was by design and our face to face changed my life. The Lord has confirmed much through his teaching, which has contributed to the writing of this book.

About the Author

Shawn Teats is Pastor of Eternal Life Fellowship in Stafford Springs, Connecticut. This is a small town grassroots work with a regular attendance of 15 saints and growing. God's movement is in this small congregation as He is pouring out His gifts. Shawn has studied Christian Ministry at Hope International University's Apostolic School of Theology. Prior to starting Eternal Life Fellowship, Shawn has served in various capacities of ministry in churches domestically and in Europe. He has studied prophecy for over twenty years and has been leading prophecy Bible studies for over five years.

Introduction

The rapture of the church is perhaps the most awaited hour of Christianity and perhaps one of the most disputed events. The irony is that scripture never mentions the word rapture but the event is accounted for in other language. It is referred to as the day of the Lord, the catching away, the resurrection, the second coming, and the gathering of the elect. It is the time when the Lord Jesus Christ will return to redeem His church out of this world. So, what is the mystery? What is the dispute?

Like many things in scripture, the rapture is clouded in mystery. In the modern world, the events surrounding the rapture, to include the rapture itself, makes for great cinema and story. A picture of cataclysmic destruction and agony strike fear and anxiety in the heart of the hearer. Couple that with confusion to its timing and sequence in events leads to a misunderstanding of the times that Jesus said we are supposed to know. People like the shroud of mystery and inconclusive understanding. It tickles the ears of those who seek to have a divine revelation of these events and perpetuates the interests of the seemingly unknown.

End time prophecy existed from the beginning and as we read throughout the Old Testament we find many scriptures that pertain to those times. Nearly one-third of the Bible discusses prophecy so its importance is significant. It seems that the Lord wanted us to know something. This is what He told His disciples.

> *Ye have heard how I said unto you, I go away, and come again unto you. If ye loved me, ye would rejoice, because I said, I go unto the Father: for my Father is greater than I. And now I have told you before it come to pass, that, when it is come to pass, ye might believe. (John 14:28-30)*

Jesus spoke of His ascension to Heaven and His return from Heaven, the rapture. He said that He tells us things before they happen so when they happen, we might believe. His disciples worried about His going away but He reassured them of His return and as we look at what Jesus said throughout His ministry, He was not shy about discussing His return.

After studying the Word and prophecy for many years, I know this truth. There is no doubt as we see the world shaping up today that the events discussed throughout scripture are happening. The news headlines are saying the same thing that scripture foretold and it builds my faith. It is so clear that those who profess Christianity around the world see that the prophecies are coming to pass. There seems to be a stirring among believers that Jesus Christ is getting ready to return. There is no doubt in their minds of this truth. The problem is the confusion surrounding end time prophecies and there doesn't have to be.

While writing this book I was very careful to use scripture and nothing but scripture. Anything outside of scripture is opinion. I don't want opinion. I want to know what God has to say about these topics. The popular view of end time events sees it one way and in their view it as absolute, even if the possible shows another way. I wrote this book on tribulation and rapture so we can see what the Bible says. I hope to show you truth through scripture. You must evaluate that for yourself through study and prayer. This work has much scripture in it because people tend not to look up references. I encourage you, have your Bible with this book and look it up for yourself. We can know certain things by looking at the scriptures and we can understand with confidence how things will happen, to a certain degree. That's why God gave it to us, so we can know the signs of the time.

Chapter 1

Signs of the Times

Signs of the Times

Jesus did not leave us blind to anything. He was open about everything He taught. He hid nothing and when people asked questions, He answered them. We find through the gospels that the disciples asked Him many questions and one of those was the time frame of His return. One thing that must be understood is with His first coming many missed it. They didn't discern the times. Jesus chastised them for this.

> *The Pharisees also with the Sadducees came, and tempting desired him that he would shew them a sign from heaven. He answered and said unto them, When it is evening, ye say, It will be fair weather: for the sky is red. And in the morning, It will be foul weather to day: for the sky is red and lowring. O ye hypocrites, ye can discern the face of the sky; but can ye not discern the signs of the times? A wicked and adulterous generation seeketh after a sign; and there shall no sign be given unto it, but the sign of the prophet Jonas. And he left them, and departed. (Matthew 16:1-4)*

Jesus told us the signs are there and we must discern them. He stated that we could know the times we are in. We find that often with many areas of our walk where we ask for a sign, yet the signs are there. This was true of His first coming and it also pertains to His second coming.

There are signs all around us and they are leading to the time when Jesus returns. There are things to look for so we can see the season. Jesus gave us this so we don't fall into deception. There is much warning in scripture, not only from Jesus, but also from the Apostles about false prophets and false Christs, confirming what Jesus had said. They are to come into the world and their job is deception. The enemy of our souls has always sought to copy God because he wants

2

to be God and he can't. There is one God and the devil hates that and he hates whoever follows the ways of the Lord.

The devil's attack on the people of God has been seen since Adam and Eve and their fall in the Garden of Eden. He has sought to put a blemish on humanity since God created us, and that will continue until his judgment. Some of his tactics are discussed through this book because knowing how the enemy works may help us avoid deception. The only way to do so is by understanding the truth and we can understand them.

> *And I heard, but I understood not: then said I, O my Lord, what shall be the end of these things? And he said, Go thy way, Daniel: for the words are closed up and sealed till the time of the end. Many shall be purified, and made white, and tried; but the wicked shall do wickedly: and none of the wicked shall understand; but the wise shall understand. (Daniel 12:8-10)*

This passage speaks of the time of the end. Daniel, a mighty prophet of God, sought to understand the visions he was having. God told him that these things are sealed and reserved for the people of the time of the end. Since that time, people have sought to figure things out and bring understanding to end time events but God told us understand won't come until a certain time. The wonderful thing is the time is upon us and we are seeing these events unfold before our eyes. While I can't discuss all the signs from the Bible in this book, I will discuss a few of them to show we are in the time of the end. If you want to understand the signs in the Bible, take the time to study it. This book's intent is to wet the appetite for further study of God's word.

There are clues throughout scripture with phrases such as "in the last days". Jesus gave us these clues so we can know the generation we are in and how to handle it. God gives each generation the capacity to handle the times in which they live. He raises up preachers, teachers, and prophets to confirm His word to the generation He wishes to speak. The term prophet seems archaic and Old Testament like, but prophets are still used by the Lord. As we witness in the Bible, as sure as there are prophets, there will be false prophets and scripture has many warnings about the increase of false prophets in the last days.

> *For there shall arise false Christs, and false prophets, and shall shew great signs and wonders; insomuch that, if it were possible, they shall deceive the very elect. (Matthew 24:24)*

This will lead to an individual person who will convince the world to worship a man often referred to as the antichrist. The man who convinces the world to do so is called the false prophet. Leading to that there will be many false prophets and false Christs and this warns us to discern them.

Many people in Christianity today are afraid to cast judgment on anyone, yet Jesus gave us these warnings so we can discern them and tell whether they are sent to speak truth or sent to spread deception. To judge nothing is a ridiculous notion and has created the condition of the church today. Sin is running rampant through congregations that profess the name of Jesus Christ and when sin is challenged people contend that we shouldn't judge. How can a Christian survive in the modern world if he isn't allowed to judge sin? There is a certain amount of judgment that we are supposed to do. Discernment tells us the intent of the person or circumstance and it is how we can war against deception.

> *And he said, Take heed that ye be not deceived: for many shall come in my name, saying, I am Christ; and the time draweth near: go ye not therefore after them. (Luke 21:8)*

Here we see that Jesus was warning us again about deception and false Christs. This is an end time prophecy because in this chapter Jesus discusses tribulation and His return. He told us to take heed so we are not deceived. He said people would come in His name. He is telling us to judge these people to see if they are from God. It is imperative we judge what people say and what they do so we don't fall into the snare of deception.

> Beloved, believe not every spirit, but try the spirits whether they are of God: because many false prophets are gone out into the world. (1 John 4:1)

The Apostle John, who was also one of the twelve disciples of Jesus, confirmed what the Lord said that we are to try the spirits to see whether they are of God. This is discerning people's intentions and that is judgment so do not be afraid to judge because salvation may depend on it.

There is clear instruction from our Lord that we are to watch out for false prophets and false Christs but scripture alludes to several conditions of the people of the last days that will allow these false prophets to have voice.

> This know also, that in the last days perilous times shall come. For men shall be lovers of their own selves, covetous, boasters, proud, blasphemers, disobedient to parents, unthankful, unholy, Without natural affection, trucebreakers, false accusers, incontinent, fierce, despisers of those that are good, Traitors, heady, highminded, lovers of pleasures more than lovers of God; Having a form of godliness, but denying the power thereof: from such turn away. For of this sort are they which creep into houses, and lead

*captive silly women laden with sins, led away
with divers lusts, Ever learning, and never able
to come to the knowledge of the truth. (2
Timothy 3:1-7)*

Here we see how evil will take over the condition of
people's hearts. This is sin having its way in the world
and the people of that time will fall for it. This
condition is a reprobate society where they will love the
evils and pleasures of this world than the truth of God's
word. It is a society that thinks itself to know better
than what God has to say. Does this sound familiar?
We see this upon us now and it will get worse.

It is this thinking that changes the condition of
society. Sin runs rampant and the people become deaf
to the truth. People choose leaders full of compromise
and error, yet they are celebrated to be progressive and
understanding the needs of the people. These leaders
make laws that will change the lives of the people but
not for the better. Freedoms get taken away and power
shifts from the people, who once walked in the fear of
the Lord, to the rulers who intend total control and
power. They demonize people who bring common
sense and truth and praise people who lean toward sin
and compromise. This is true of the general condition
of society but we find also true of the church and that is
where it gets dangerous.

*For the time will come when they will not
endure sound doctrine; but after their own lusts
shall they heap to themselves teachers, having
itching ears; And they shall turn away their
ears from the truth, and shall be turned unto
fables. (2 Timothy 4:3-4)*

This is speaking of the church and it says the
time will come when they will not endure sound
doctrine. We see that today. It is amazing the things
that people believe that are contrary to what scripture
says. They have turned their ears from the truth of

6

God's word and have turned to fables and false doctrine. Also, the teachers that are teaching the false doctrine have itching ears. They love to hear their congregations tell them how wonderful the message was today, and it made them feel good. Feel good messages do not get people saved or keep them saved. It feeds their lusts so they can continue in their ways without conviction. They support these false teachers because of no conviction. I know from experience, when the truth is preached and conviction comes to someone, they must choose. They either repent from their wicked deeds or they get mad at the preacher for preaching the message.

People today like the feel good messages of prosperity and abundant life here on earth. The Lord spoke of persecution, trouble in this world, and not trusting in the riches of this world but in the world to come. We are taught to separate ourselves from this world because this world and this life will pass and we will face eternity. I would rather build up my eternity than the things of this life. Jesus taught us we must give up this life and the things of it to gain salvation in the next life. But itchy-eared teachers will propagate this message of prosperity and riches in this life and congregations support them by the droves. Yet, you find sin and perversion entering the church and the pulpit. Ministers are falling into all kinds of vile and disgusting sins that are celebrated in the world today.

> *Knowing this first, that there shall come in the last days scoffers, walking after their own lusts, And saying, Where is the promise of his coming? for since the fathers fell asleep, all things continue as they were from the beginning of the creation. (2 Peter 3:3-4)*

We see this occurring in the world. I have heard people say, "They've been saying for two-thousand years that Jesus is coming back and He hasn't yet"! This is a direct sign of this prophecy and a sign of the last days. The problem is that when people think along these lines, they feel justified in regressing toward sin. Their faith fades because they don't believe that what the Bible says will happen. This is due to a lack of patience because the world wants everything and they want it now. We have to be careful not to grow impatient because Jesus has a plan of salvation and His grace has not run out yet. He is long-suffering toward us because a gospel must be preached and people need to hear it.

Matthew 24 gives an excellent prophecy of the condition of the world in the last days prior to Christ's return. It is the words of our Lord Jesus Christ and His timeline of the end. This prophecy (Mark 13 and Luke 21 also give this prophecy) is the Lord's prophecy so we need to pay attention to it. Jesus is God so God Himself was telling us the chronology of events that would precede His return. This is an end time prophecy and there is a way to know that.

> *And Jesus went out, and departed from the temple: and his disciples came to him for to shew him the buildings of the temple. And Jesus said unto them, See ye not all these things? verily I say unto you, There shall not be left here one stone upon another, that shall not be thrown down. And as he sat upon the mount of Olives, the disciples came unto him privately, saying, Tell us, when shall these things be? and what shall be the sign of thy coming, and of the end of the world? (Matthew 24:1-3)*

The disciples were trying to show Jesus the temple because it was a magnificent building but Jesus told them that not one stone would be left on the other and the temple would fall. The disciples asked first, "when shall these things be"? From history we know that happened in 70 A.D. when the Roman General Titus took Jerusalem and cast down the temple, fulfilling this prophecy. The second question asked was "and what

8

shall be the sign of thy coming, and of the end of the world"?

Jesus told them the signs that would lead up to His return at the end of the age. When inquiring about the end of the world, they were asking about the end of the age. Scripture tells us after His return there will be a thousand years of reign on this earth before He recreates everything (Revelation 20:5-7, Revelation 21:1). So, the discussion is not the end of the world but the end of the age of human government and the ushering in of the Kingdom of God ruled by Jesus Christ (Revelation 11:14).

There are events that precede His return and specific events He said to watch.

> *And Jesus answered and said unto them, Take heed that no man deceive you. For many shall come in my name, saying, I am Christ; and shall deceive many. And ye shall hear of wars and rumours of wars: see that ye be not troubled: for all these things must come to pass, but the end is not yet. For nation shall rise against nation, and kingdom against kingdom: and there shall be famines, and pestilences, and earthquakes, in divers places. All these are the beginning of sorrows. (Matthew 24:4-8)*

In answering the questioning of timing, Jesus expounded on things that lead up to how the last days will look. Here we see a general condition of events we could say has been happening for some time now. Some of these things happened in the early church but we are seeing them happen again today and will cause a time worse than what the early church experienced. Jesus warned us not to be deceived because there will be people that will come in His name to deceive. Just because someone slaps the Christian label on something that doesn't mean it is Christian.

That may strike a nerve with those who believe that anyone who says they are Christian is one. Many

9

of the biggest warnings in the Bible concern false prophets and false Messiahs. Recent history has shown that many people claim to be Jesus or a type of messiah. In the convolution of truth the world is experiencing, no wonder that people fall for the deception. They are so deceived that they won't heed this exact prophecy that was written over two thousand years ago. Yet, they still need proof the Bible is true.

Remember, Jesus told us *And now I have told you before it come to pass, that, when it is come to pass, ye might believe. (John 14:30)* This should be enough proof that the Bible is true. Events are playing out how the Bible states they would and every single prophecy in the Bible will come to pass. The bible does not need the church to prove its legitimacy. The church just needs to preach the truth that is written in its pages. It will prove itself and that is why prophecy is given so when it happens, people may believe.

After this, Jesus spoke of a worsening condition of hatred toward believers.

> *Then shall they deliver you up to be afflicted, and shall kill you: and ye shall be hated of all nations for my name's sake. And then shall many be offended, and shall betray one another, and shall hate one another. And many false prophets shall rise, and shall deceive many. And because iniquity shall abound, the love of many shall wax cold. But he that shall endure unto the end, the same shall be saved. (Matthew 24:9-13)*

He said then they shall deliver you up to be afflicted, they shall kill you, and you shall be hated of all nations for my name's sake. This is where the world is at right now. The world is seeing the beheadings and persecutions of Christians in many nations. The antichristian rhetoric is also prevalent in a country that prides itself on religious freedom – The United States.

This is another sign of the times in the world. This is not something we are waiting for. It is happening. As the Lord said, Christians will see betrayals by loved ones because of the offense of Christianity. The gospel offends because people want to live any way they wish and the truth won't let them so they have to destroy it. It might surprise you that is also true in Christian circles. This is where the false prophets come in and they try to portray another way to salvation contrary to scripture. Those who hold to the Bible are persecuted for standing on the truth they know.

A sign of the times is that Christians will hold to this truth no matter what the world is saying.

> *Be it known unto you all, and to all the people of Israel, that by the name of Jesus Christ of Nazareth, whom ye crucified, whom God raised from the dead, even by him doth this man stand here before you whole. This is the stone which was set at nought of you builders, which is become the head of the corner. Neither is there salvation in any other: for there is none other name under heaven given among men, whereby we must be saved. (Acts 4:10-12)*

The goal of the world government (United Nations) and the world religions is to say all religions offer a valid pathway to salvation. They say you worship God in your way, I worship in my way, and we are worshipping the same God. If you profess Christianity and believe that, you are walking in a lie. The Bible states that Jesus Christ is the only name by which we can be saved. There is no salvation in any other.

That Christians believe that Jesus Christ is the only way to salvation is the reason for their persecution. Christian principle flies in the face of a world government that has an agenda to unite the world through politics, spirituality, and economics. This is the picture of tribulation for the Christian. Revelation 13 depicts this with precision because the first beast mentioned is the system of the antichrist. The second beast is the system of the false prophet and the last section of the chapter deals with the "mark of the beast", the economic system of the one world government. The mark of the beast will also be the vehicle to enforce tribulation on Christians. So these are the signs of the times the world is in right now. Now, we have to see what's ahead.

Chapter 2

The Great Tribulation

The Great Tribulation

This is the most feared event in Christianity. For centuries people have been trying to find its meaning. Some see a way of escape so this time does not have to be endured. They have also believed this is the wrath of God being poured out on the world because of the wickedness that dominates society. Others can't imagine the atrocities that will take place and even try to deny its reality.

There are three schools of thought on this event. Most believe the church is raptured before great tribulation (pre-trib). Others believe that the church will endure part of it then be taken half way through (mid-trib), yet others believe that the church will endure it and then receive reward for not giving into the antichrist system of the world (post-trib). But, what does scripture say? What matters is we must adhere to scripture in all things and accept the plan of God no matter what His word says.

This is not meant to cause contention or to fly in the face of anyone's theology. I think most people are genuine in their beliefs and most of the time teachers teach the things they've learned from others. They perpetuate their theology because they trust the people they who taught them. So what this does is perpetuate a teaching whether true or not. Most people being taught rely on the knowledge of the teacher rather than studying the scriptures and finding out what is true. All three opposing beliefs of tribulation and rapture of the church can't be true.

Also, I have no special knowledge or insight other than what the Bible teaches. That's where I look and even in the authoring of this book I am conflicted. I don't think it's necessary because the Bible tells you everything you need to know. I am tempted to quote other works but the word of God speaks for itself and does not need embellishment. So, I will stake my claim on the word of God and the word of God alone. The only reason I write this book is as an avenue to preach the truth and since many would rather read books about the Bible than the Bible itself, I am receiving the unction from the Holy One to speak against the deception in the world. Also, I once held to a certain belief on this until scripture taught me the truth. As with everything I teach, this will be full of scripture and not man's opinion. It's the only way to live so let's see what scripture says.

> *And this gospel of the kingdom shall be preached in all the world for a witness unto all nations; and then shall the end come. When ye therefore shall see the abomination of desolation, spoken of by Daniel the prophet, stand in the holy place, (whoso readeth, let him understand:) Then let them which be in Judaea flee into the mountains: Let him which is on the housetop not come down to take any thing out of his house: Neither let him which is in the field return back to take his clothes. And woe unto them that are with child, and to them that give suck in those days! But pray ye that your flight be not in the winter, neither on the sabbath day: For then shall be great tribulation, such as was not since the beginning of the world to this time, no, nor ever shall be. And except those days should be shortened, there should no flesh be saved: but for the elect's sake those days shall be shortened. (Matthew 24:14-22)*

The Lord tells us wonderful truths here. He speaks some of what it will be like during that time and gives information concerning the timing. In a later chapter all of this will come together to show a basic timeline of how these events will play out. Scripture gives information on what to look for and what the church should do when faced with these events.

Jesus told us that the church is to do what He commissioned us to do and that is to preach the gospel. He said it would be preached in the entire world as a

15

witness to all nations and then the end shall come so even during tumultuous times the church of Jesus Christ needs to preach the gospel. That is the vision we need to grasp. Once we understand that vision then it becomes our mission or "commission" as we have labeled it. The devil is famous for causing chaos and distraction to prevent the church from filling its commission. Most of us can attest to this on a personal level and this will ascend into a corporate level as the church faces tribulation. Contrary to the what people say, the church will be a church of power during that time because it's the last offensive before we leave this world. When in history has God lost to the devil? The answer is NEVER!

Now we can get a glimpse of tribulation. Jesus told us it would be a time of great tribulation such as never was nor ever again shall be. So the world has not seen this yet. Not to the scale that will be during that time. The early church endured tribulation. There is no doubt about that but Jesus said that this time is more troublesome than that of the early church. The reason for that may vary. Perhaps greater because it will be worldwide and more Christians are in the world than before. It could also be because the evil of man's heart has waxed worse over the centuries but scripture gives a superb reason this is the case.

> *And there was war in heaven: Michael and his angels fought against the dragon; and the dragon fought and his angels, And prevailed not; neither was their place found any more in heaven. And the great dragon was cast out, that old serpent, called the Devil, and Satan, which deceiveth the whole world: he was cast out into the earth, and his angels were cast out with him. And I heard a loud voice saying in heaven, Now is come salvation, and strength, and the kingdom of our God, and the power of his Christ: for the accuser of our brethren is cast down, which accused them before our God day*

and night. And they overcame him by the blood of the Lamb, and by the word of their testimony; and they loved not their lives unto the death. Therefore rejoice, ye heavens, and ye that dwell in them. Woe to the inhabiters of the earth and of the sea! for the devil is come down unto you, having great wrath, because he knoweth that he hath but a short time. And when the dragon saw that he was cast unto the earth, he persecuted the woman which brought forth the man child. And to the woman were given two wings of a great eagle, that she might fly into the wilderness, into her place, where she is nourished for a time, and times, and half a time, from the face of the serpent. And the serpent cast out of his mouth water as a flood after the woman, that he might cause her to be carried away of the flood. And the earth helped the woman, and the earth opened her mouth, and swallowed up the flood which the dragon cast out of his mouth. And the dragon was wroth with the woman, and went to make war with the remnant of her seed, which keep the commandments of God, and have the testimony of Jesus Christ. (Revelation 12:7-17)

This passage answers many questions. It gives the reason and the source of great tribulation to the people of God. The devil can go before the throne and accuse the brethren. At some point God will put an end to this and this causes a war to happen where the archangel Michael will battle the devil and his demons until they are cast out of heaven. This will cause the devil to have great wrath and he will turn that wrath towards the people of God. This is the great tribulation and if you read verse 17 you will see through other scriptures that the great tribulation affects the Jewish people and the church.

So, one question answered is that the great tribulation is not the wrath of God. It is the wrath of the devil because he is cast out of heaven. There is a school of thought out there that the church can't be here for the great tribulation because God would never pour His wrath out on His church. It s true that God won't pour out His wrath on the church but the great tribulation is not the wrath of God. It is the wrath of Satan. The devil is wroth with the woman in Revelation 12, which is Israel, and he goes to make war with the remnant of her seed, those that keep the commandments of God (Jews) and have the testimony of Jesus Christ (Christians).

There is another thing to point out beginning in verse 10. This is in the midst of the tribulation hour and here it says that *"Now is come salvation, and strength, and the kingdom of our God, and the power of his Christ: for the accuser of our brethren is cast down, which accused them before our God day and night. And they overcame him by the blood of the Lamb, and by the word of their testimony; and they loved not their lives unto the death"*. This shows that even though the devil's influence will increase in this world because of his wrath and the drive to make war with the people of God, that God's power will also increase in His people. That the church will have to run scared is false and so as we venture through this difficult topic, we will also see encouragement because we will have power and strength during that time. Remember, the church must still fulfill its commission all the way until the end.

While we are on what the great tribulation is, let's explore more of what scripture tells us. Revelation 12 starts by describing the great tribulation as a time of trouble. *And at that time shall Michael stand up, the great prince which standeth for the children of thy people: and there shall be a time of trouble, such as never was since there was a nation even to that same time: and at that time thy people shall be delivered, every one that shall be found written in the book. (Revelation 12:1)* The first question that may be asked is how can we know this is speaking of the great tribulation. John tells us "there shall be a time of trouble, such as never was since there was nation even to that time". Jesus told us a similar thing in Matthew 24. *For then shall be great tribulation, such as was not since the beginning of the world to this time, no, nor ever shall be. (Matthew 24:21)* Since this happens once, John is speaking of the time of great tribulation spoken by the Lord Jesus.

So, it will be a time of trouble. After all it is the great tribulation so it will time where God's people are tested. There will be persecution and the Lord's description in Matthew 24 alludes to that. Revelation 12 describes this as the devil's wrath against God's people and other scriptures show of a time where the man of sin will make war against the saints. *I beheld, and the same horn made war with the saints, and prevailed against them; Until the Ancient of days came, and judgment was given to the saints of the most High; and the time came that the saints possessed the kingdom. (Daniel 7:21-22)* The little horn is the antichrist, the man of sin, the son of perdition, or whatever name that is associated with him or his kingdom. He will make war with the saints so there will be a campaign against the saints of God with the intending to eliminate them.

> *And there was given unto him a mouth speaking great things and blasphemies; and power was given unto him to continue forty and two months. And he opened his mouth in blasphemy against God, to blaspheme his name, and his tabernacle, and them that dwell in heaven. And it was given unto him to make war with the saints, and to overcome them: and power was given him over all kindreds, and tongues, and nations. (Revelation 13:5-7)*

Seen here is another description of the war he will make against the saints of God but we see some other clues here that need to be discussed. The timing of this event will be shown in a later chapter; however, it says here he will have power over the saints for forty-

19

two months. There is a teaching in the world that there will be seven years of tribulation, yet seen in this passage and in others, antichrist rule will be half of that.

Also seen in this passage is a very important clue. He opens his mouth in blasphemy against God, to blaspheme God's name, tabernacle, and them that dwell in heaven. This describes an event known as the "Abomination of Desolation" and it is something that Jesus warned us to watch for. Just before the Lord's description of the great tribulation, He said to watch for this event because it will trigger the great tribulation. *When ye therefore shall see the abomination of desolation, spoken of by Daniel the prophet, stand in the holy place, (whoso readeth, let him understand:) (Matthew 24:15)* Jesus said watch for this event because once you see it; you will see great tribulation beginning in Judea and then form other passages we know that it will spread through the world.

Jesus said Daniel the prophet spoke of it so what did Daniel say?

> *And he shall confirm the covenant with many for one week: and in the midst of the week he shall cause the sacrifice and the oblation to cease, and for the overspreading of abominations he shall make it desolate, even until the consummation, and that determined shall be poured upon the desolate. (Daniel 9:27)*

Daniel describes seventy weeks that will pertain to from the going forth of the commandment to rebuild Jerusalem all the way to the crowning of our Lord Jesus Christ. The final week described in Daniel 9:27 shows two major events. What begins the week is a peace agreement with Israel and the international community concerning borders, Jerusalem, and the temple mount. In the midst of that week the abomination of desolation is established. This event triggers great tribulation. This will be clearer in a later chapter but it had to be mentioned now.

Jesus told us it would happen in the holy place alluding to the temple mount in a Jewish temple that will reside there. Revelation 13:6 says that the antichrist will blaspheme God and His tabernacle. John describes a blasphemous event in the temple. The Apostle Paul describes what this event is.

> *Now we beseech you, brethren, by the coming of our Lord Jesus Christ, and by our gathering together unto him, That ye be not soon shaken in mind, or be troubled, neither by spirit, nor by word, nor by letter as from us, as that the day of Christ is at hand. Let no man deceive you by any means: for that day shall not come, except there come a falling away first, and that man of sin be revealed, the son of perdition; Who opposeth and exalteth himself above all that is called God, or that is worshipped; so that he as God sitteth in the temple of God, shewing himself that he is God. (2 Thessalonians 2:1-4)*

This is the abomination of desolation and this is the event the Lord Jesus says we will see which will lead into great tribulation where the devil will use the man of sin, the antichrist, to make war with the saints of God.

And he had power to give life unto the image of the beast, that the image of the beast should both speak, and cause that as many as would not worship the image of the beast should be killed. (Revelation 13:15) The journey through Revelation 13 shows of a second beast representing the system of the false prophet who will cause the world to worship the first beast representing the system of the antichrist. Verse 15 shows that those who do not worship the antichrist or his system should be killed. This worries many people and causes fear in their hearts. The last day's church will see persecution similar to that of the early church. Yet, they remained

21

strong because they lived by faith and the church today must live by faith.

> *And what shall I more say? for the time would fail me to tell of Gedeon, and of Barak, and of Samson, and of Jephthae; of David also, and Samuel, and of the prophets: Who through faith subdued kingdoms, wrought righteousness, obtained promises, stopped the mouths of lions, Quenched the violence of fire, escaped the edge of the sword, out of weakness were made strong, waxed valiant in fight, turned to flight the armies of the aliens. Women received their dead raised to life again: and others were tortured, not accepting deliverance; that they might obtain a better resurrection: And others had trial of cruel mockings and scourgings, yea, moreover of bonds and imprisonment: They were stoned, they were sawn asunder, were tempted, were slain with the sword: they wandered about in sheepskins and goatskins; being destitute, afflicted, tormented; (Of whom the world was not worthy:) they wandered in deserts, and in mountains, and in dens and caves of the earth. And these all, having obtained a good report through faith, received not the promise: God having provided some better thing for us, that they without us should not be made perfect. (Hebrews 11:32-40)*

When thinking great tribulation many think of a fearful time or a powerless time. Revelation 12 describes that during this God's power will be on His church but as we progress through this topic, we will see where the church will be in power and not in fear during great tribulation. Things described in this passage, despite the political correctness and tolerance mentality of the world today, will happen. The truth about tolerance means let's tolerate everyone who agrees with us, others we will demonize. The true church of Jesus Christ will not cave to the ridiculous notions of tolerance and political correctness and that will be where tribulation stems from. To buy into it means the church has to compromise the Word of God. If you will compromise that, then you don't belong to the church.

Hebrews 11 describes heroes of faith. When we read verses 33 through the end of the chapter we see a description of how the early church was persecuted. These men and women stood in faith despite the circumstances surrounding them. They were not willing to compromise the truth for anything, not even their lives. In fact, scripture describes the tribulation under the fifth seal.

> *And when he had opened the fifth seal, I saw under the altar the souls of them that were slain for the word of God, and for the testimony which they held: And they cried with a loud voice, saying, How long, O Lord, holy and true, dost thou not judge and avenge our blood on them that dwell on the earth? And white robes were given unto every one of them; and it was said unto them, that they should rest yet for a little season, until their fellowservants also and their brethren, that should be killed as they were, should be fulfilled. (Revelation 6:9-11)*

This shows two major periods of time. John saw souls under the altar in heaven waiting for their blood to be avenged. They were promised yet a little season because there will be saints who must be killed as they were. This is the great tribulation. Revelation 12:11 tells us *And they overcame him by the blood of the Lamb, and by the word of their testimony; and they loved not their lives unto the death.* So under no circumstance is it okay to bow to the antichrist and false prophet systems and there is a special place in heaven for those who remain true and give their lives for the truth.

One other way tribulation will be carried out is also described in Revelation 13.

> *And he causeth all, both small and great, rich and poor, free and bond, to receive a mark in their right hand, or in their foreheads: And that no man might buy or sell, save he that had the mark, or the name of the beast, or the number of his name. Here is wisdom. Let him that hath understanding count the number of the beast: for it is the number of a man; and his number is Six hundred threescore and six. (Revelation 13:16-18)*

There are many theories that surround the mark of the beast that would be too numerous to discuss in this setting but here is what we can know. It involves the economic system of the antichrist rule. It will be used to persecute the church even in places the antichrist can't reach them. You will not be able to buy or sell unless you have this mark and some will fall because of that. Under no circumstance is the church to take the mark of the beast. This spells eternal damnation for those that do.

> *And the third angel followed them, saying with a loud voice, If any man worship the beast and his image, and receive his mark in his forehead, or in his hand, The same shall drink of the wine of the wrath of God, which is poured out without mixture into the cup of his indignation; and he shall be tormented with fire and brimstone in the presence of the holy angels, and in the presence of the Lamb: And the smoke of their torment ascendeth up for ever and ever: and they have no rest day nor night, who worship the beast and his image, and whosoever receiveth the mark of his name. (Revelation 14:9-11)*

To buy into the antichrist system and to accept his mark will mean eternal suffering in the lake of fire and that torment will ascend up forever. There is no repentance for those who take the mark. There is so much warning about this in the Bible that there will be no excuse for those that bow down to the world government system where this mark will come from. To accept it means to turn your back on God and worship the beast. The church will not do so and this causes tribulation. The church will antagonize the antichrist because it won't play by his rules. We can see the beginnings of it now.

Here is the patience of the saints: here are they that keep the commandments of God, and the faith of Jesus. (Revelation 14:12) Tribulation works patience. Paul told us in Romans 5:3 that tribulation works patience. In fact, he said to glory in tribulations knowing they work patience. Leaning on God through our trials now helps us have patience to endure tribulation and great tribulation when it comes on the world. Here is the patience of the saints we endure tribulation and not cave to another way when things get difficult. We are people of faith and we are justified by faith. That means in the face of persecution and loving not our lives unto death.

There is one final point about great tribulation to end this discussion on a good note. We will have power and Daniel gives us some information to help us during that time.

> *And arms shall stand on his part, and they shall pollute the sanctuary of strength, and shall take away the daily sacrifice, and they shall place the abomination that maketh desolate. And such as do wickedly against the covenant shall he corrupt by flatteries: but the people that do know their God shall be strong, and do exploits. And they that understand among the people shall instruct many: yet they shall fall by the sword, and by flame, by captivity, and by spoil,*

25

many days. Now when they shall fall, they shall be holpen with a little help: but many shall cleave to them with flatteries. And some of them of understanding shall fall, to try them, and to purge, and to make them white, even to the time of the end: because it is yet for a time appointed. (Daniel 11:31-35)

This happens in the great tribulation because this passage mentions the abomination of desolation followed by persecution of the saints but verses 32 and 33 tell us what we need to do. They that know their God shall be strong and do exploits and they that have understanding among the people shall instruct many. It is a time of power to those that know God and a time of use for those who have understanding. The church will not bow in fear nor will it fall without a fight. The church will prevail and if we must give our lives for the Lord, we will enter into eternity to be with Him. There is no losing for the people of God. The tribulation is about a temper tantrum that the devil throws because he is kicked out of heaven once and for all. It is a time of spiritual warfare on a monumental level and it will take strong soldiers of Christ who live their lives by faith to endure. The warning is be ready! Know God and learn His word so we can be a formidable foe to the devil during the time of great tribulation so we can fulfill our Great Commission!

Chapter 3

The Same Evil

The Same Evil

If they persecuted those in the early church for preaching the gospel why wouldn't the end time church go through the same peril? Scripture points out in so many places that will be the case, but why is it that modern people think this way? Perhaps we have become so "enlightened" and humanity has progressed beyond the savagery of persecuting people? If you believe that, take a look at Holocaust or more recently, the beheadings of Christians in the Middle East. It will only be on a grander scale and instead of men's hearts being "enlightened", they have been blinded by iniquity and hatred. It is the same evil at work today as in the first century. It is the same evil that has continuously persecuted the people of God since time began.

To understand this point, we must take a look at origins of antichrist and his kingdom.

> *In the first year of Belshazzar king of Babylon Daniel had a dream and visions of his head upon his bed: then he wrote the dream, and told the sum of the matters. Daniel spake and said, I saw in my vision by night, and, behold, the four winds of the heaven strove upon the great sea. And four great beasts came up from the sea, diverse one from another. The first was like a lion, and had eagle's wings: I beheld till the wings thereof were plucked, and it was lifted up from the earth, and made stand upon the feet as a man, and a man's heart was given to it. And behold another beast, a second, like to a bear, and it raised up itself on one side, and it had three ribs in the mouth of it between the teeth of it: and they said thus unto it, Arise, devour much flesh. After this I beheld, and lo another, like a leopard, which had upon the back of it four wings of a fowl; the beast had also four heads; and dominion was given to it. After this I saw in the night visions, and behold a fourth*

*beast, dreadful and terrible, and strong
exceedingly; and it had great iron teeth: it
devoured and brake in pieces, and stamped the
residue with the feet of it: and it was diverse
from all the beasts that were before it; and it
had ten horns. I considered the horns, and,
behold, there came up among them another
little horn, before whom there were three of the
first horns plucked up by the roots: and, behold,
in this horn were eyes like the eyes of man, and
a mouth speaking great things. (Daniel 7:1-8)*

Daniel saw a vision of beasts as symbols. These beasts
rising lead to the kingdom of the man we refer to as the
antichrist. As with many prophecies, there are symbols
that are used here that would confuse the reader if there
were no idea what they could be. Since God is not the
author of confusion, He has given clues what these
symbols represent. The good news is for this prophecy;
we need not look very far.

*I Daniel was grieved in my spirit in the midst of
my body, and the visions of my head troubled
me. I came near unto one of them that stood by,
and asked him the truth of all this. So he told
me, and made me know the interpretation of the
things. These great beasts, which are four, are
four kings, which shall arise out of the earth.
But the saints of the most High shall take the
kingdom, and possess the kingdom for ever,
even for ever and ever. Then I would know the
truth of the fourth beast, which was diverse
from all the others, exceeding dreadful, whose
teeth were of iron, and his nails of brass; which
devoured, brake in pieces, and stamped the
residue with his feet; And of the ten horns that
were in his head, and of the other which came
up, and before whom three fell; even of that
horn that had eyes, and a mouth that spake very
great things, whose look was more stout than*

29

his fellows. I beheld, and the same horn made war with the saints, and prevailed against them; Until the Ancient of days came, and judgment was given to the saints of the most High; and the time came that the saints possessed the kingdom. Thus he said, The fourth beast shall be the fourth kingdom upon earth, which shall be diverse from all kingdoms, and shall devour the whole earth, and shall tread it down, and break it in pieces. And the ten horns out of this kingdom are ten kings that shall arise: and another shall rise after them; and he shall be diverse from the first, and he shall subdue three kings. And he shall speak great words against the most High, and shall wear out the saints of the most High, and think to change times and laws: and they shall be given into his hand until a time and times and the dividing of time. (Daniel 7:15-25)

Daniel asked for interpretation of the visions he had, and God told him what these things mean. This confirms that these kingdoms will culminate with the kingdom of the antichrist in power. The saints will possess the kingdom but not until the Ancient of Days returns and gives the power of the kingdom to His saints. The Ancient of Days being our Lord and God, Jesus Christ. Until then, we see from this passage that the fourth beast will speak blasphemy against God and seek to wear out His saints. The saints shall be given into his hand for a time, times, and a dividing of time.

The key then is what do these symbols mean? What are these beasts? Daniel tells us through the interpretation that God gave him these beasts represent kings and kingdoms. Verse 17 states the four beasts are kings that rise up out of the earth. Verse 23 states that the fourth beast shall be the fourth kingdom on earth. So, the beasts represent nations and rulers of those nations. In understanding what these nations are help us to understand where the antichrist will rise from since he is the little horn that speaks great words against the Most High.

Today we use animal symbols for nations so it should be no surprise that Daniel saw animals as symbols of nations. Also, this passage shows us these nations must be present in order for the antichrist kingdom rises. We can understand what these nations are by taking a look at the descriptions God gave to Daniel regarding them. God gave them and people of the end time would understand their meaning because it is the people of the end time that would be impacted by them. This describes the kingdom of the antichrist so God was reaching the people that would see it.

The first was like a lion, and had eagle's wings: I beheld till the wings thereof were plucked, and it was lifted up from the earth, and made stand upon the feet as a man, and a man's heart was given to it. (Daniel 7:4) There are two nations mentioned here. Daniel saw a lion with eagle's wings. He beheld as the wings were plucked from the lion. On July 4, 1776 this prophecy was fulfilled as The United States of America, whose national symbol is the eagle, declared independence from Great Britain, whose national symbol is the lion. In declaring her independence, the United States fought a brutal war to gain it; therefore the eagle's wings were forcefully removed (plucked) from the lion. Once plucked the eagle's wings became a separate symbol, and it was made to stand on two feet like a man and a man's heart was given to it. America has another national symbol that is a man and that is Uncle Sam. This passage plays out perfectly with how history describes the formation of the United States, which is significant, because these nations must exist for the rest of this prophecy to be fulfilled.

And behold another beast, a second, like to a bear, and it raised up itself on one side, and it had three ribs in the mouth of it between the teeth of it: and they said thus unto it, Arise, devour much flesh. (Daniel 7:5) The nation described here has a bear as its symbol. It is a strong nation and uses military might to

31

conquer so the question that has to be asked is whether any nation today has a bear as its national symbol and a strong military. The answer is Russia, and she has been flexing her military might through the twentieth century and is resurfacing as a military superpower in the twenty-first century.

After this I beheld, and lo another, like a leopard, which had upon the back of it four wings of a fowl; the beast had also four heads; and dominion was given to it. (Daniel 7:6) This nation's primary symbol is also an eagle, but God is not the author of confusion so God called out another symbol this nation uses and that is the leopard. This nation also has four dominions so it is a nation that will rise and fall four times. It has been strong three times historically and is now the strong economic power in Europe. This nation is Germany. We have seen the first three Reich's rise and fall and of course the most well known being Hitler's third Reich. The economic rise to power is being dubbed as the fourth Reich.

Germany has had powerful dominion throughout the Holy Roman Empire and she has had powerful dominion during the twentieth century. History records her as being responsible for the start of both World Wars. Her unofficial national symbol is the leopard, or panther. Her most feared weapon of war is the Panzer tank. To reiterate, the black eagle is her official symbol. The leopard is her unofficial symbol and as this chapter develops, you will see something particular to this nation in Revelation 13. But, first let's look at what else Daniel says.

> *After this I saw in the night visions, and behold a fourth beast, dreadful and terrible, and strong exceedingly; and it had great iron teeth: it devoured and brake in pieces, and stamped the residue with the feet of it: and it was diverse from all the beasts that were before it; and it had ten horns. I considered the horns, and, behold, there came up among them another*

32

little horn, before whom there were three of the
first horns plucked up by the roots: and, behold,
in this horn were eyes like the eyes of man, and
a mouth speaking great things (Daniel 7:7-8)

Daniel tells us this fourth beast is dreadful and terrible. It is strong and relentless and will devour and break in pieces. This beast is ruthless in its pursuit and there is nothing on earth that will stop it. This is a picture of the kingdom of the antichrist. We see a common description of the antichrist himself as a little horn and how he will speak great things against the Most High.

As you continue in Daniel 7, this terrible and dreadful beast will reign until the Ancient of days establishes His kingdom here on earth. Of course, this is talking about our Lord and God, Jesus Christ and He will return to establish His kingdom on earth. However, until that happens, and once the antichrist takes power, he will be given dominion until the Lord returns. His absolute control is from the time of the Abomination of Desolation until the Lord's return, however, according to Daniel 9:27, he will be in the background facilitating agreements with Israel and the world community. He will also be setting up his rise to power and given the condition of the world, it is very plausible that he is alive now and the world is just waiting for the right time for his rise to power.

Daniel 7 illustrates a point that the nations represented are nations that must be on the earth during the time of the final kingdom that will rise just before the return of the Lord. It was not possible for this to come to pass until the United States came to be, which is represented by the eagle's wings standing on two feet like a man. Daniel saw these as separate beasts but John saw them differently in his vision in Revelation 13.

And I stood upon the sand of the sea, and saw a
beast rise up out of the sea, having seven heads
and ten horns, and upon his horns ten crowns,
and upon his heads the name of blasphemy.

And the beast which I saw was like unto a leopard, and his feet were as the feet of a bear, and his mouth as the mouth of a lion: and the dragon gave him his power, and his seat, and great authority. And I saw one of his heads as it were wounded to death; and his deadly wound was healed: and all the world wondered after the beast. And they worshipped the dragon which gave power unto the beast: and they worshipped the beast, saying, Who is like unto the beast? who is able to make war with him? And there was given unto him a mouth speaking great things and blasphemies; and power was given unto him to continue forty and two months. And he opened his mouth in blasphemy against God, to blaspheme his name, and his tabernacle, and them that dwell in heaven. And it was given unto him to make war with the saints, and to overcome them: and power was given him over all kindreds, and tongues, and nations. And all that dwell upon the earth shall worship him, whose names are not written in the book of life of the Lamb slain from the foundation of the world. (Revelation 13:1-8)

This passage represents the kingdom of the antichrist and from it we see familiar beasts. The lion, bear, and leopard are all represented here and so it is the ten-horned beast out of Daniel 7. John saw those beasts as one kingdom, which is represented by the seven heads and ten horns. All of the seven heads and ten horns are from Daniel's vision, just combined into one kingdom in John's vision. This is significant as Daniel states that out of this kingdom emerges the antichrist.

Another important truth is the kingdom of the antichrist is not ruled only by the antichrist. Revelation 13 says there is another that is in power that will cause the world to worship the beast, and that person is called the False Prophet.

*And I beheld another beast coming up out of
the earth; and he had two horns like a lamb,
and he spake as a dragon. And he exerciseth all
the power of the first beast before him, and
causeth the earth and them which dwell therein
to worship the first beast, whose deadly wound
was healed. And he doeth great wonders, so
that he maketh fire come down from heaven on
the earth in the sight of men, And deceiveth
them that dwell on the earth by the means of
those miracles which he had power to do in the
sight of the beast; saying to them that dwell on
the earth, that they should make an image to the
beast, which had the wound by a sword, and did
live. And he had power to give life unto the
image of the beast, that the image of the beast
should both speak, and cause that as many as
would not worship the image of the beast should
be killed. (Revelation 13:11-15)*

The first half of Revelation 13 shows the beast (the
kingdom of the antichrist) will be worshipped.
Remember, beasts represent kingdoms and their rulers
so it is the antichrist that is worshipped along with his
kingdom. Verse 11 states that a second beast will rise
causing all to worship the first beast. This second beast
will do so by false miracles and great wonders. So, the
question then becomes, what type of beast is this?

The answer is in verse 11: *And I beheld another
beast coming up out of the earth; and he had two horns
like a lamb, and he spake as a dragon.* This gives a
clear description of what this beast is. The description
says it has two horns like a lamb, and he speaks as a
dragon. Putting another way, he looks like a lamb but
speaks like a dragon and so then the symbolism used
must be cleared up. This is easy to do within scripture.
There is no guessing what a lamb and a dragon
represent so where do we find out to be sure?

From scripture you can know the lamb represents Jesus Christ. You don't have to leave the book of Revelation to discover that.

> *And I beheld, and, lo, in the midst of the throne and of the four beasts, and in the midst of the elders, stood a Lamb as it had been slain, having seven horns and seven eyes, which are the seven Spirits of God sent forth into all the earth. And he came and took the book out of the right hand of him that sat upon the throne. And when he had taken the book, the four beasts and four and twenty elders fell down before the Lamb, having every one of them harps, and golden vials full of odours, which are the prayers of saints. (Revelation 5:6-8)*

This passage discusses an image of a slain lamb, full of the seven Spirits of God, and when He had taken the book, the 24 elders fell down to worship Him. This is Jesus Christ and if there is any doubt, John the Baptist gave a similar description of Jesus. *The next day John seeth Jesus coming unto him, and saith, Behold the Lamb of God, which taketh away the sin of the world. (John 1:29)* So, the lamb in Revelation 13 looks like Christianity but it also speaks like a dragon.

Again, you don't have to leave Revelation to know what the dragon is. You have to look in the previous chapter to find that meaning and to know what is being represented here.

> *And there was war in heaven: Michael and his angels fought against the dragon; and the dragon fought and his angels, And prevailed not; neither was their place found any more in heaven. And the great dragon was cast out, that old serpent, called the Devil, and Satan, which deceiveth the whole world: he was cast out into the earth, and his angels were cast out with him. (Revelation 12:7-9)*

36

It states in plain language what the dragon is. It is the Devil, and Satan, who deceives the whole world. So, the second beast will look like Christ, or Christianity, but will speak like Satan. What does that mean? The False Prophet will come from a false Christian system but will be a figure that many think represents Christianity. He will perform miracles and lying signs and wonders but they are done to deceive. They will be there to cause the world to follow the Antichrist and his world government system.

What you see here is a marriage between the political system and the religious system. In fact it will be a repeat of a system that has already existed and one that the world is seeing rise again and as you might have guessed, it is happening how the Bible shows. This next prophecy travels through time beginning with ancient Babylon and prophesying all the way until the Ancient of Days is seated in His Kingdom.

> *The king answered and said to Daniel, whose name was Belteshazzar, Art thou able to make known unto me the dream which I have seen, and the interpretation thereof? Daniel answered in the presence of the king, and said, The secret which the king hath demanded cannot the wise men, the astrologers, the magicians, the soothsayers, shew unto the king; But there is a God in heaven that revealeth secrets, and maketh known to the king Nebuchadnezzar what shall be in the latter days. Thy dream, and the visions of thy head upon thy bed, are these; As for thee, O king, thy thoughts came into thy mind upon thy bed, what should come to pass hereafter: and he that revealeth secrets maketh known to thee what shall come to pass. But as for me, this secret is not revealed to me for any wisdom that I have more than any living, but for their sakes that shall make known the interpretation to the king,*

and that thou mightest know the thoughts of thy heart. Thou, O king, sawest, and behold a great image. This great image, whose brightness was excellent, stood before thee; and the form thereof was terrible. This image's head was of fine gold, his breast and his arms of silver, his belly and his thighs of brass, His legs of iron, his feet part of iron and part of clay. Thou sawest till that a stone was cut out without hands, which smote the image upon his feet that were of iron and clay, and brake them to pieces. Then was the iron, the clay, the brass, the silver, and the gold, broken to pieces together, and became like the chaff of the summer threshingfloors; and the wind carried them away, that no place was found for them: and the stone that smote the image became a great mountain, and filled the whole earth. This is the dream; and we will tell the interpretation thereof before the king. Thou, O king, art a king of kings: for the God of heaven hath given thee a kingdom, power, and strength, and glory. And wheresoever the children of men dwell, the beasts of the field and the fowls of the heaven hath he given into thine hand, and hath made thee ruler over them all. Thou art this head of gold. And after thee shall arise another kingdom inferior to thee, and another third kingdom of brass, which shall bear rule over all the earth. And the fourth kingdom shall be strong as iron: forasmuch as iron breaketh in pieces and subdueth all things: and as iron that breaketh all these, shall it break in pieces and bruise. And whereas thou sawest the feet and toes, part of potters 'clay, and part of iron, the kingdom shall be divided; but there shall be in it of the strength of the iron, forasmuch as thou sawest the iron mixed with miry clay. And as the toes of the feet were part of iron, and part of clay, so the kingdom shall be partly strong, and

*partly broken. And whereas thou sawest iron
mixed with miry clay, they shall mingle
themselves with the seed of men: but they shall
not cleave one to another, even as iron is not
mixed with clay. And in the days of these kings
shall the God of heaven set up a kingdom, which
shall never be destroyed: and the kingdom shall
not be left to other people, but it shall break in
pieces and consume all these kingdoms, and it
shall stand for ever. Forasmuch as thou sawest
that the stone was cut out of the mountain
without hands, and that it brake in pieces the
iron, the brass, the clay, the silver, and the
gold; the great God hath made known to the
king what shall come to pass hereafter: and the
dream is certain, and the interpretation thereof
sure. (Daniel 2:26-45)*

There is a lot here but Daniel was interpreting a
dream for Nebuchadnezzar that was troubling his mind.
He knew he had a dream but couldn't remember it and
knew that it was important so he called on his wise men
and astrologers to make known the dream and
interpretation. They could not answer so they asked
Nebuchadnezzar to tell them the dream and they would
interpret. Nebuchadnezzar was wiser than that and
understood they would make up an interpretation even
if he could tell them the dream, but he didn't'
remember it. The wise men then retorted by saying this
is too much of a thing for the king to ask of his servants
and this enraged the king so he sent out a decree to
have all the wise men of the land killed.

Daniel was told of this decree and asked the
king's captain to allow audience with the king and it
was granted. Daniel asked Nebuchadnezzar to give him
some time and he would not only give him the
interpretation of the dream but also the dream itself.
Daniel prayed and God gave the dream and the
interpretation to Daniel. Daniel went in before
Nebuchadnezzar and answered his request.

Daniel stated that this was a latter day prophecy and what God was showing was the age of empires that should come upon the earth from that time until the end. He saw an image which had a head of gold, arms and chest of silver, belly and thighs of brass, legs of iron, feet of iron mingled with clay. Daniel watched a stone cut out of a mountain and rolled down and smashed the feet of the image and destroyed the image and the stone grew into a great mountain and filled the earth. The king assured Daniel that was the dream and then Daniel gave interpreted the dream.

Daniel pointed out that the head of Gold was Nebuchadnezzar, the king of Babylon. The arms and chest of silver was a kingdom inferior to Babylon that would overcome Babylon and assume its place as an empire. The belly and thighs of brass was another kingdom that would come after to rule the world. The legs of iron were strong and mighty and they would rule with the strength of iron. The feet of iron mingled with clay would rule after that and would be partly strong with iron and partly broken with clay. These two would not cleave to each other as iron can't mix with clay.

If the head is Babylon, then look at history to see what happened, thus making Daniel a book where history was written in advance and giving testimony that the Bible is true. The truth is that the Bible also shows historically what happened. History books will show what the Bible already knew and you don't have to look very far to see whom the arms and chest of silver represent.

> *And this is the writing that was written, mene, mene, tekel, upharsin. This is the interpretation of the thing: mene; God hath numbered thy kingdom, and finished it. tekel; Thou art weighed in the balances, and art found wanting. peres; Thy kingdom is divided, and given to the Medes and Persians. Then commanded Belshazzar, and they clothed Daniel with*

*scarlet, and put a chain of gold about his neck,
and made a proclamation concerning him, that
he should be the third ruler in the kingdom. In
that night was Belshazzar the king of the
Chaldeans slain. And Darius the Median took
the kingdom, being about threescore and two
years old. (Daniel 5:25-31)*

The arms and chest of silver represent the Medes and
Persians who took the kingdom from Babylon because
of the arrogance of Nebuchadnezzar's son Belshazzar.
Belshazzar wanted to impress his guests at a feast and
used the Jewish temple vessels taken in captivity from
Jerusalem and God was not pleased. So, the
handwriting on the wall (Mene, Mene, Tekel, Upharsin)
was by the hand of God and Belshazzar could not
understand it. Daniel's reputation preceded him and he
was called to interpret this. Daniel gave the
interpretation that Babylon would cease to be a
kingdom that night and it came to pass.
    Daniel also tells who should replace Media-
Persia as represented by the belly and thighs of brass.

*In the third year of the reign of king Belshazzar
a vision appeared unto me, even unto me
Daniel, after that which appeared unto me at
the first. And I saw in a vision; and it came to
pass, when I saw, that I was at Shushan in the
palace, which is in the province of Elam; and I
saw in a vision, and I was by the river of Ulai.
Then I lifted up mine eyes, and saw, and,
behold, there stood before the river a ram which
had two horns: and the two horns were high;
but one was higher than the other, and the
higher came up last. I saw the ram pushing
westward, and northward, and southward; so
that no beasts might stand before him, neither
was there any that could deliver out of his hand;
but he did according to his will, and became
great. And as I was considering, behold, an he*

41

*goat came from the west on the face of the
whole earth, and touched not the ground: and
the goat had a notable horn between his eyes.
And he came to the ram that had two horns,
which I had seen standing before the river, and
ran unto him in the fury of his power. And I saw
him come close unto the ram, and he was moved
with choler against him, and smote the ram, and
brake his two horns: and there was no power in
the ram to stand before him, but he cast him
down to the ground, and stamped upon him:
and there was none that could deliver the ram
out of his hand. Therefore the he goat waxed
very great: and when he was strong, the great
horn was broken; and for it came up four
notable ones toward the four winds of heaven.
(Daniel 8:1-8)*

Daniel had a vision from the palace at Shushan, which
was the Persian capital. In this vision, he was by the
river Ulai and saw a ram with two horns. This ram was
strong and had dominion toward the west, the north,
and the south. Daniel then saw a goat, which had a
notable horn and the goat charged the ram with power
and smote the ram breaking its two horns; therefore
breaking its power. So, the question is who do the ram
and the goat represent?

Daniel gives the answer to this question. *The
ram which thou sawest having two horns are the kings
of Media and Persia. And the rough goat is the king of
Grecia: and the great horn that is between his eyes is
the first king. (Daniel 8:20-21)* Daniel states the ram is
Media and Persia and the goat is Greece and history
records as Alexander the Great (represented by the
great horn of the goat) moved with might and power
and conquered the known world by the time he was
thirty years old and he defeated Media-Persia during his
conquests so the belly and thighs of brass from Daniel 2
represent Greece.

The legs of iron are not hard to figure out. History records that the Roman Empire defeated the Greek Empire around 241 B.C. during the Punic Wars that started due to Rome's expanding influence throughout the Mediterranean. Rome's influence was strong and throughout its existence, held a strong military might. They conquered by military power and they held domination of known world for five hundred years. This is why iron represents Rome, because of its strength. While this piece of history isn't written in the Bible as the other three empires in Nebuchadnezzar's dream, the evidence of Rome's power is shown in the New Testament.

> *And it came to pass in those days, that there went out a decree from Caesar Augustus, that all the world should be taxed. (And this taxing was first made when Cyrenius was governor of Syria.) And all went to be taxed, every one into his own city. And Joseph also went up from Galilee, out of the city of Nazareth, into Judaea, unto the city of David, which is called Bethlehem; (because he was of the house and lineage of David:) To be taxed with Mary his espoused wife, being great with child. And so it was, that, while they were there, the days were accomplished that she should be delivered. And she brought forth her firstborn son, and wrapped him in swaddling clothes, and laid him in a manger; because there was no room for them in the inn. (Luke 2:1-7)*

Augustus Caesar was the first emperor of Rome. He was reigning when Jesus Christ was born and we know that Jesus spoke with Roman soldiers throughout His ministry. Jesus stood trial before Pontius Pilate who was the Roman prefect in Judea and the early Christian church suffered persecution under the Roman emperors.

Now, as you turn your attention to the feet of Daniel 2, there are two things that many look over but they are very significant. Before that is revealed, Bible prophecy is given to keep the church steady in perilous times. When you look at the world, or even people in the church that don't bother with prophecy, there is imaginative speculation about the future and sometimes this speculation plants fear in the hearts of men. The reason this is mentioned here is because the feet of iron mingled with clay is such a prophecy that not only helps to understand not only how the antichrist kingdom comes about but also gives specific clues where the antichrist himself will come from.

So, the first thing is to examine the feet and see what Daniel says concerning them.

> *And whereas thou sawest the feet and toes, part of potters 'clay, and part of iron, the kingdom shall be divided; but there shall be in it of the strength of the iron, forasmuch as thou sawest the iron mixed with miry clay. And as the toes of the feet were part of iron, and part of clay, so the kingdom shall be partly strong, and partly broken. And whereas thou sawest iron mixed with miry clay, they shall mingle themselves with the seed of men: but they shall not cleave one to another, even as iron is not mixed with clay. And in the days of these kings shall the God of heaven set up a kingdom, which shall never be destroyed: and the kingdom shall not be left to other people, but it shall break in pieces and consume all these kingdoms, and it shall stand for ever. (Daniel 2:41-44)*

This part of the prophecy is the first time that an element of the previous empire is carried over to the next empire. Remember, the legs made of iron, and since the iron is the Roman Empire then an element of the Roman Empire is carried over to the next empire, however there is another element mixed in and that is

44

the clay. The prophecy says that the mixture of iron and clay causes the feet to be partly strong and partly broken and that the two elements of this empire will not cleave to each other because iron can't mix with clay.

The question to ask is has there ever been an empire in history that has retained an element of Rome and had another element thrown in that had dominion and rule? The answer is yes but many don't realize this was the case because they don't think of this empire as one of the great empires. In fact, this empire has lasted longer than the other four. The span of this empire lasted just over one thousand years, which is twice as long as the Roman Empire. From 800 A.D. to 1806 A.D. the Holy Roman Empire ruled in Europe.

How does the Holy Roman Empire fit the prophecy of the feet of iron mingled with clay? The element of the iron is the political rule of an emperor. It has been since Daniel spoke to Nebuchadnezzar stating that he was the head of gold. The element describes the king and their kingdom. An emperor, starting with Augustus Caesar, ruled Rome. Yes, Rome had a senate and for a long time democracy ruled but as it gained power and began conquests, an emperor ruled the empire. This element carried on to the Holy Roman Empire when Pope Leo III crowned Charlemagne first emperor of the Holy Roman Empire in A.D. 800. The first element is political.

The second element is the religious element because throughout the Holy Roman Empire, rule was shared. There were matters of state and then matters of church. The religious element is the clay of Daniel's prophecy. They would be in agreement as long as their power didn't interfere with one another. Once either the Pope or the Emperor thought his power was greater, there would be problems and wouldn't cleave to one another. To recap, the feet of iron mingled with clay represent the Holy Roman Empire where the political leader (Emperor) was the iron and the religious leader (Pope) was the clay and they would not cleave together as one wanted to usurp their authority over the other.

Something else that many miss in this prophecy is the feet have toes called out separately. *And whereas thou sawest the feet and toes, part of potters 'clay, and part of iron, the kingdom shall be divided; but there shall be in it of the strength of the iron, forasmuch as thou sawest the iron mixed with miry clay. (Daniel 2:41)* The toes play an important role in the prophecy. They are called out separately for a reason. The thing to remember with the toes is that they are part of the feet but being identified as toes shows that they are an entity all their own, however, they come from the same mixture the feet come from. This indicates a revival of the Holy Roman Empire. It is in this resurgence of the Holy Roman Empire where the antichrist will rise and the Lord Jesus Christ will return to establish His kingdom. *And in the days of these kings shall the God of heaven set up a kingdom, which shall never be destroyed: and the kingdom shall not be left to other people, but it shall break in pieces and consume all these kingdoms, and it shall stand for ever. (Daniel 2:44)* When speaking of kings of end time prophecy there are several references to ten kings.

The seven headed ten horned beast discussed earlier is a represents the ten kingdom system.

> *And the ten horns out of this kingdom are ten kings that shall arise: and another shall rise after them; and he shall be diverse from the first, and he shall subdue three kings. And he shall speak great words against the most High, and shall wear out the saints of the most High, and think to change times and laws: and they shall be given into his hand until a time and times and the dividing of time. (Daniel 7:24-25)*

Remember, this is the same beast described in Revelation 13, which are a conglomerate beast from the lion, bear, leopard, and the fourth beast that Daniel saw as separate beasts. There is a ten-horned kingdom that arises out of whom the antichrist will assume power.

This is what the toes in Daniel 2 represent and when these ten kings take power the world can know that the Lord's return is near.

Daniel's prophecy shows history written in advance by describing the rise and fall of world empires ending up with the rebirth of the Holy Roman Empire where the antichrist (political leader) and the false prophet (religious leader) will rule the final world empire. It will be the same way the Holy Roman Empire ran for one thousand years, except with more veracity because Satan himself will give dominion to this system as described in Revelation 13. One other prophecy pertinent to this discussion can be found in Revelation 17.

> *And there came one of the seven angels which had the seven vials, and talked with me, saying unto me, Come hither; I will shew unto thee the judgment of the great whore that sitteth upon many waters: With whom the kings of the earth have committed fornication, and the inhabitants of the earth have been made drunk with the wine of her fornication. So he carried me away in the spirit into the wilderness: and I saw a woman sit upon a scarlet coloured beast, full of names of blasphemy, having seven heads and ten horns. And the woman was arrayed in purple and scarlet colour, and decked with gold and precious stones and pearls, having a golden cup in her hand full of abominations and filthiness of her fornication: And upon her forehead was a name written, Mystery, Babylon the Great, the Mother of harlots and abominations of the earth. And I saw the woman drunken with the blood of the saints, and with the blood of the martyrs of Jesus: and when I saw her, I wondered with great admiration. And the angel said unto me, Wherefore didst thou marvel? I will tell thee the mystery of the woman, and of the beast that carrieth her,*

which hath the seven heads and ten horns. The beast that thou sawest was, and is not; and shall ascend out of the bottomless pit, and go into perdition: and they that dwell on the earth shall wonder, whose names were not written in the book of life from the foundation of the world, when they behold the beast that was, and is not, and yet is. And here is the mind which hath wisdom. The seven heads are seven mountains, on which the woman sitteth. And there are seven kings: five are fallen, and one is, and the other is not yet come; and when he cometh, he must continue a short space. And the beast that was, and is not, even he is the eighth, and is of the seven, and goeth into perdition. And the ten horns which thou sawest are ten kings, which have received no kingdom as yet; but receive power as kings one hour with the beast. These have one mind, and shall give their power and strength unto the beast. These shall make war with the Lamb, and the Lamb shall overcome them: for he is Lord of lords, and King of kings: and they that are with him are called, and chosen, and faithful. (Revelation 17:1-14)

This is a prophecy of the Mystery Babylon and how her integration with the end time world government will seek to control the world and to make war with the saints of God. It shows the relationship of the worldview of the political and religious agenda. The key to this is to understand what we learned so far because it shows another angle of how the revived Holy Roman Empire rules. There are seven kings. Five have fallen, one is, and the other is not yet come, but when he comes, he continues for a short time. The beast that was, and is not, is the eighth, but of the seven and he goes into perdition.

What does this even mean? In light of what was learned already it is simple to figure out. This is John's vision of Daniel's prophecy of empires. It is from

John's point in time as Daniel's was from his point in time. Daniel was looking fro Babylon onward. John was looking from Rome backward and then prophesying of the future rise of the antichrist government. The seven kings with five fallen. In John's day the Roman Empire was at its height so in this prophecy the Roman Empire is the one that is.

So who are the five that were fallen? Daniel gives us understanding of three of them and they are Babylon, Media-Persia, and Greece. Now before Babylon, there were two other powerful empires that Israel had to contend with. These empires were active even when Israel and Judah went into captivity. These are known as Egypt and Assyria so the five that are fallen from John's viewpoint are Egypt, Assyria, Babylon, Media-Persia, and Greece. John was alive during the Roman Empire so that is the sixth or as John states, the one that is. The seventh is the Holy Roman Empire and that was yet to come from John's time and there is an eighth kingdom, which is of the seven. This is the revived Holy Roman Empire, and it is this kingdom that will go into perdition producing the kingdom of the antichrist and the false prophet.

Why the term Mystery Babylon? This is a pertinent discussion for this topic on the same evil because the evil root lies where Babylon originated. The word Babylon originated from the word Babel. 2 Kings 17:24 in the King James Version of the Bible is the very first time Babylon is mentioned. Looking at the Strong's Concordance the Hebrew term Babylon is the same as the term Babel. It means confusion and Babel is the root of Babylon. The significance of Babel is that God gave a command but man decided not to trust God's word and do things his own way. It was a subtle but defiant action against the Lord.

> *And the whole earth was of one language, and of one speech. And it came to pass, as they journeyed from the east, that they found a plain in the land of Shinar; and they dwelt there. And*

they said one to another, Go to, let us make brick, and burn them throughly. And they had brick for stone, and slime had they for morter. And they said, Go to, let us build us a city and a tower, whose top may reach unto heaven; and let us make us a name, lest we be scattered abroad upon the face of the whole earth. And the Lord came down to see the city and the tower, which the children of men builded. And the Lord said, Behold, the people is one, and they have all one language; and this they begin to do: and now nothing will be restrained from them, which they have imagined to do. Go to, let us go down, and there confound their language, that they may not understand one another's speech. So the Lord scattered them abroad from thence upon the face of all the earth: and they left off to build the city. Therefore is the name of it called Babel; because the Lord did there confound the language of all the earth: and from thence did the Lord scatter them abroad upon the face of all the earth. (Genesis 11:1-9)

Genesis 10:9-10 describes who the leader of Babel was and his name was Nimrod who was a mighty hunter before the Lord. He was a descendent of Noah. He was a son of Cush, who was a son of Ham, who was a son of Noah and he was a mighty hunter before the Lord. This means he knew God but God desired something of mankind after Noah left the ark.

And God blessed Noah and his sons, and said unto them, Be fruitful, and multiply, and replenish the earth. (Genesis 9:1) God instructed Noah and his sons to replenish the earth, which meant they were to spread out and fill the earth. Babel was a direct defiance to God's instruction. Because the people were of one language they conspired against the commandment of God and built a high tower to become a people lest they be scattered abroad upon the face of the earth. God confused the language and the people were scattered

50

throughout the earth. The point here is Nimrod and his people knew the Lord. They knew of the flood and they knew what was expected of them but they made a decision to do things their way and caused false religion to come into God's recreation of the earth.

This false religious ideology exists in the end time world system. As learned previously, it will look like Christianity but speak like the devil. This is why the term Mystery Babylon is used. As John describes, she is the Mother of Harlots and abominations of the earth. It is interesting that since Babel is the root for Babylon, the defiance against God in political and religious circles is growing increasingly in the modern world. This idea is flowing so easily in the hearts of men and ultimately the Judeo-Christian persecution will come from it. Just like it did throughout the ages and just like in the early church. It truly is the same evil that has been there all along.

Chapter 4

The Apostasy

The biggest reason people shy away from thought of persecution is fear. As you try to teach what the Bible says about great tribulation and how the church will endure it, people immediately fear. In fact, this is used sometimes as a reason to dispute the validity of the claim. People think that if it makes you afraid then it must not be from God. People fear what will happen to them more than what God can do through them. They fear the world more than they fear God. Why? It is because love is not perfected in them. *There is no fear in love; but perfect love casteth out fear: because fear hath torment. He that feareth is not made perfect in love. We love him, because he first loved us. (1 John 4:18-19)*

Persecution for our faith is downplayed or even disregarded in society today. We have adapted to easy living and easy faith. People are quickly drawn to faith that is lacking in purity. Any tribulation is seen as the person's lack of faith, which is completely opposite of the truth. The preaching in today's mainstream church is very unnerving as it represents a false view of Christian living. I'm not denying God's blessings but the idea of what has been dubbed as the "prosperity gospel" waters down truth. It views blessing as reward and tribulation as something bad, yet Paul gloried in tribulation (Romans 5:3). Tribulation can also be a blessing because it causes us to rely on God. *Yea, and all that will live godly in Christ Jesus shall suffer persecution. (2 Timothy 3:12)*

The gospel preached today is built on an easy faith. Many preachers are preaching that the Christian doesn't need to suffer. Some are saying that if a person is suffering there must be sin in his life. To many Christians, suffering is something that has negative connotations and many avoid Spirit led paths because they may have some sort of tribulation associated with them. Instead, they follow paths that seem easy and view them as the will of God. In reality, some of these easy paths are far from the will of God. This is not to say that blessing is out of God's will but what are we counting as blessing? Does being blessed mean being rich? Does it mean having big houses or fancy cars? Does it mean that we can divorce until we find a spouse that is "compatible" with us? Then are we blessed?

Even the reading of these words will cause some to get their feathers ruffled because they will take offense that the easy life does not mean they are blessed. They will justify their lifestyles by saying "God wants me to be happy". They make foolish decisions by believing that God wouldn't expect anything bad to happen to them. Many are so accustomed to this way of thinking that any bit of persecution is unimaginable to them. It is a selfish way of thinking and when persecution comes their way, they react to it like a spoiled child.

They want no measure of judgment passed to them when they continue in their ungodly lifestyles. When a brother lovingly points out their sinful action, they say, "Judge not lest ye be judged", basing it from where Jesus made that statement in the gospels. *Judge not, that ye be not judged. (Matthew 7:1)* It is a wonder that they can quote scriptures that justify their actions but they can't comprehend what Jesus was saying as you read on.

> *For with what judgment ye judge, ye shall be judged: and with what measure ye mete, it shall be measured to you again. And why beholdest thou the mote that is in thy brother's eye, but considerest not the beam that is in thine own eye? Or how wilt thou say to thy brother, Let me pull out the mote out of thine eye; and, behold, a beam is in thine own eye? Thou hypocrite, first cast out the beam out of thine own eye; and then shalt thou see clearly to cast out the mote out of thy brother's eye. (Matthew 7:2-5)*

Jesus was not telling us we shouldn't judge. He was telling us that if we are to make judgment, we better have our own walk in order. How can a brother instruct in righteousness if he is not living righteously himself? A drug addict can't cast judgment on a drunkard if they haven't overcome their own addiction. A preacher can't tell a brother that his adulterous relationship is wrong if he had an affair on his own wife and married his mistress. In this age of anything goes, people have accepted ungodly behavior and when someone preaches truth, they are persecuted and chastised for the truth they bring. Most of the time all they are doing is showing scripture, but the defenses go up and instead of repenting of sinful ways, the person would rather take offense.

These are real issues that ministers deal with and it is because of the worldly mindset that the church has adopted. Since when is the church supposed to look like the world? This is a huge problem. How is the church supposed to witness to the world if they look like the world or perhaps even worse? There is something wrong with the present condition of the church when they won't adhere to sound doctrine and righteous instruction in holiness. How can the church lead to righteousness if it doesn't offer a better way of life? A life that pleases the Lord is heading toward the kingdom of God. If you are trying to please this world, you will not make the kingdom of God. *Ye adulterers and adulteresses, know ye not that the friendship of the world is enmity with God? whosoever therefore will be a friend of the world is the enemy of God. (James 4:4)*

The church has to get away from worldly thinking and actions. These actions make us the enemy of God. Most of Christianity is falling away from the truth and making excuses for it. The warning is to be sure you don't follow them. There is a way that pleases the Lord and that is what must be sought. This way would be a shock to most people today. You hear it in their comments as things happen. "My God would never allow something like that to happen"! My response to that is, have you read your Bible? That's where it has to start. Since most are following seducing spirits and doctrines of devils, then the place to go would be to the Bible, which is instruction from God on how to live for Him.

Many people say, "It's just a book written by men" or "It needs to catch up with the times". It is more than a book; it is scripture. This means it is to be followed because scripture is given by God through men to instruct in holy living. *All scripture is given by inspiration of God, and is profitable for doctrine, for reproof, for correction, for instruction in righteousness: That the man of God may be perfect, throughly furnished unto all good works. (2 Timothy 3:16-17)* This means that the Christian must be malleable to scripture, no matter what it says. You can't change scripture or its meaning to fit a lifestyle contrary to God. You can't water down scripture to justify your sin. God has always called out sin and He still does so today. If it was sin in the Old Testament, it's sin now. If it was sin in the early church, it's sin now. The only difference between the Old and New Testaments is how that sin is judged. The New Testament affords the believer an opportunity to change his ways for sin condemned under the law.

In a world that wants to live its own way, these words almost become illegal. If a preacher speaks against sinful lifestyles, he is marked as a legalist or extremist. People don't want their lifestyle to be judged and you can understand that for the world. They know not what they do but it becomes dangerous for the church. There are heresies going on in the church that are wretched and gross sin that's not Christianity. It is time for the church to hold itself accountable and get back to Biblical truths and stop caving to devilish doctrines. If the church can adopt a Biblical mindset, then it will correct itself through the word of God and living holy unto the Lord. There is coming a separation of true Christianity from apostasy. Apostasy is false

Christianity and unfortunately, it dominates Christian thinking today.

> *Now the Spirit speaketh expressly, that in the latter times some shall depart from the faith, giving heed to seducing spirits, and doctrines of devils; Speaking lies in hypocrisy; having their conscience seared with a hot iron; Forbidding to marry, and commanding to abstain from meats, which God hath created to be received with thanksgiving of them which believe and know the truth. For every creature of God is good, and nothing to be refused, if it be received with thanksgiving: For it is sanctified by the word of God and prayer. If thou put the brethren in remembrance of these things, thou shalt be a good minister of Jesus Christ, nourished up in the words of faith and of good doctrine, whereunto thou hast attained. But refuse profane and old wives'fables, and exercise thyself rather unto godliness. For bodily exercise profiteth little: but godliness is profitable unto all things, having promise of the life that now is, and of that which is to come. This is a faithful saying and worthy of all acceptation. For therefore we both labour and suffer reproach, because we trust in the living God, who is the Saviour of all men, specially of those that believe. These things command and teach. (1 Timothy 4:1-11)*

The Apostle Paul gave strong warning concerning the days we live in. This is the latter time and many are departing from the faith. Church membership has decreased in recent years and people follow other things to fill the gap. They do command to abstain from meats, both in church circles and in secular circles. Sin has dominated holy thought because people have no regard for right and wrong. Their consciences are seared with a hot iron. The condition of the church today is such that the gospel is not even preached anymore. People are taught that all you have to do is believe and nothing else. This has caused a false sense of salvation because the ministry is not instructing in sound doctrine. Sound doctrine must line up with the Bible since that is the word of God.

It is important that the church understands truth and how to live it to prevent her from falling into apostasy. Aside from what Paul stated here, there are devilish doctrines that are circulating the world causing Christians to fall away from the faith. These doctrines seem like they are the direction to go in but they take people away from God. They attempt to diminish the deity of God and deny the power of Jesus Christ. John told us that this is antichrist. *Who is a liar but he that denieth that Jesus is the Christ? He is antichrist, that denieth the Father and the Son. (1John 2:22)* People won't say this is what they do but in the guise of tolerance, ecumenism, and interfaith beliefs this is what they do.

The Bible teaches us that Jesus Christ is the only way to salvation, yet the interfaith movement teaches us that there are multiple pathways to God. They say people can worship any god or no god at all. While it is a person's right to do so, this school of thought is dangerous! In fact, this is the most dangerous thought of the 21st Century. Especially in the guise of an ambitious campaign to diminish the truth that Jesus Christ is the only way to salvation and to reject the infallibility of the Bible, which the Christian understands to be the word of God.

> *Be it known unto you all, and to all the people of Israel, that by the name of Jesus Christ of Nazareth, whom ye crucified, whom God raised from the dead, even by him doth this man stand here before you whole. This is the stone which was set at nought of you builders, which is become the head of the corner. Neither is there salvation in any other: for there is none other*

*name under heaven given among men, whereby
we must be saved. (Acts 4:10-12)*

This passage tells us that only through Jesus
Christ can one be saved. It states that there is no other
name given among men by which one can be saved.
Yet, the interfaith and atheists movements seek to
destroy that claim. This is antichrist. This is the school
of thought that will lead to great tribulation. The reason
is that Christians will not cave to the world pressure to
deny the truth that Jesus Christ is the only way to
salvation. The apostate church will compromise this
truth and many other truths that Christianity teaches. At
some point one has to ask when does Christianity stop
being Christian?

It appears the church is at a critical point.
Christians must decide whether they will stand on
Biblical truth or compromise that truth to where the
church will lose its identity. God won't let that happen.
People will lose their Christianity but Christianity will
prevail. It means that Christians must search out truth
and live according to it no matter what it cost. You may
have to lose family and friends. You may have to
change careers and lifestyle. You may have to look in
the mirror and decide whether you want to live
Christianity and the reward is worth any sacrifice that is
given.

Once again, this is not a popular view among
mainstream Christianity. The mainstream church is a
very secularized view that is full of compromise and
lacks in holiness. We are commanded to be holy. *But as
he which hath called you is holy, so be ye holy in all
manner of conversation; Because it is written, Be ye
holy; for I am holy. (1 Peter 1:15-16)* This is not a God
complex. This is a command by God that we make the
choice to live holy lives pleasing unto the Lord.
Holiness means to be set apart for God's service. Jesus
Christ authored salvation through His death, burial, and
resurrection so He went through lengths to sanctify us
so if we are to follow Him, why is it that we fail to

59

deny ourselves? *And he said to them all, If any man will come after me, let him deny himself, and take up his cross daily, and follow me. (Luke 9:23)* Jesus crucified His flesh to give us salvation, why is it we can't make the decision to crucify our flesh to keep our salvation?

It is a decision. The command to "be ye holy" is a command and decision we make to obey that command. The compromising church looks for loopholes so it can convince itself to look holy but in reality it is not holy. Decisions like that are made multiple times a day. Christians must adhere to what God calls holy and not what they think is holy. Just believing doesn't make you holy. *Yea, a man may say, Thou hast faith, and I have works: shew me thy faith without thy works, and I will shew thee my faith by my works. Thou believest that there is one God; thou doest well: the devils also believe, and tremble. (James 2:18-19)*

This is a clear example why belief alone is not enough. James was addressing faith and works. What he was portraying is to exercise faith, we must do so by works, or the faith is dead. Here is an example: Jesus told the lame man "rise, take up thy bed, and walk. The lame man might have believed but if he never took up his bed and walked, he would have remained a lame man. He showed his faith by his works. If you believe, you will obey what the Lord says to do. This obedience shows that you believe and now you are walking in faith.

People believe all kinds of things but that doesn't make them true. People may believe the truth and don't follow through with it so that belief is in vain. But the real danger is when someone believes a lie and they live that lie as though it is truth. The wrap it in the name of Christ and call it Christianity. There is a way for the Christian to know if he is following Biblical Christianity. Read the Bible!

There is a growing trend throughout the world where Christians are pulling away from the denominational church and finding home churches or underground churches. This is because they have opened the Bible and discovered that what their preachers are preaching does not line up with what the Bible says. It's alarming, but it is true. Preachers are watering down the faith to gain numbers in their congregations. Some feel that the truth may offend if they even see the truth. This offense will cause some to leave the flock and it is difficult for a pastor to deal with that. Some were taught a certain way, some under denominational boundaries, and they don't seek the truth because they think they have it.

For the time will come when they will not endure sound doctrine; but after their own lusts shall they heap to themselves teachers, having itching ears; And they shall turn away their ears from the truth, and shall be turned unto fables. (2 Timothy 4:3-4) This is where it gets especially dangerous and the blame goes to the teachers. This passage states that the congregations will not endure sound doctrine but because of their own lusts they raise up teachers with itching ears. Teachers with itching ears are those who love to hear how good they are. Just before this Paul told Timothy to *Preach the word; be instant in season, out of season; reprove, rebuke, exhort with all longsuffering and doctrine. (2 Timothy 4:2)* It is up to the preacher to preach God's word and not his own and sometimes the congregation will not want to hear God's word. This is where they do not endure sound doctrine because only God's word brings sound doctrine.

It should be no surprise that Christianity has fallen into this trap. The Apostle Paul prophesied what would become of the church once he left the earth. *For I know this, that after my departing shall grievous wolves enter in among you, not sparing the flock. Also of your own selves shall men arise, speaking perverse things, to draw away disciples after them. (Acts 20:29-30)* This did happen. As long as the Apostles remained, there was stability in the church. That is not to say the early church was without its problems, but the Apostles addressed it and brought truth to the lie. When they left this world, false doctrine took root and created disciples of false doctrine.

This created multiple denominations in the Christian faith. The problem is they thought they had found truth and this was the reason for the split but what happened was they continued in false teaching and the problem waxed worse and cultivated heresies seen in the modern church. It is all prophesied in the Bible and many still fail to see it. When someone comes to present Biblical truth, they are looked at as a lunatic or fanatic and dismissed by these long established denominations. It has created a condition where people don't want to go to church because they see it as hypocritical or they don't know where to go because one denomination teaches a certain way and another denomination teaches a different way so what is to be done?

Chapter 5

The Apostle's Doctrine

The Apostles' Doctrine

And they continued stedfastly in the apostles'
doctrine and fellowship, and in breaking of
bread, and in prayers. (Acts 2:42)

As previously established, the apostate church
follows false doctrine, doctrines of devils, and does not
endure sound doctrine. True doctrine was important to
the early church and the leaders of the church fought
hard to maintain the principles that Jesus Christ
established. Act 2:42 states they continued steadfastly
in the apostles' doctrine. Doctrine was taught to them
directly by Jesus Christ for the Apostles to preach
throughout the world. To understand what doctrine they
continued in you would have to read what was
happening in Acts 2. One thing to understand is
although it is commonly called *Acts* the official title is
The Acts of the Apostles. It is called that because this is
what they did and how they did it so if we continue
steadfastly in the Apostles' doctrine then this is how it
is supposed to be done today.

What happened in Acts 2? In the first chapter of
Acts, Jesus was giving final instruction before He
departed and spoke to them of the Holy Ghost and the
power they would receive once the Holy Ghost comes.
They were not to preach the gospel until this power fell
on them. Acts 2 records the power of the Holy Ghost
falling thus beginning the church age, which is sill in
existence today. This chapter tells of the day that it
happened and how the promise of God fell.

They were all in the upper room, one hundred
twenty people total. They were praying and there was a
sound of a rushing mighty wind from heaven, which
manifested in cloven tongues of fire resting on each of
their heads. Then they all spoke with tongues as the
baptism of the Holy Ghost filled them up and they were
so full they could not stay in the room any longer. They
ran outside into the streets of Jerusalem where the Bible
says there were devout men from all nations that heard

them speaking in their own native languages the wonderful works of God. The phenomenon was so pronounced that the devout men in the streets supposed them to be drunk. It was a visible and audible occurrence and all who witnessed it could see and hear.

Peter stepped out to address what was happening. He explained to them that this is the fulfillment of prophecy given to the prophet Joel concerning the outpouring of the Holy Ghost. After speaking about the fulfillment of that promise, Peter preached to them concerning Jesus Christ being the fulfillment of King David's prophecy about the resurrection of Christ. Then Peter turned the attention to the crowd who had witnessed miracles and signs and wonders wrought by God through Jesus Christ and he made the following statement: *Therefore let all the house of Israel know assuredly, that God hath made that same Jesus, whom ye have crucified, both Lord and Christ. (Acts 2:36)*

Peter revealed it was the Jewish nation, who should have known their Messiah, had Christ crucified. They witnessed God through Christ, yet they delivered Him over to be crucified. Now, this had to happen. This was God's plan so Jesus could take away the sins of the world and God used Israel to carry out that plan. It was the only way it could be done, but this caused something to happen to the hearts of the hearers. *Now when they heard this, they were pricked in their heart, and said unto Peter and to the rest of the apostles, Men and brethren, what shall we do? (Acts 2:37)* Peter's words, as with any good preaching, caused something to prick their hearts. It caused them to see they were not right with God so they asked what should we do? In other words, what must we do to get right with God? What must we do to be saved?

Peter had an immediate response. Before getting into what that response was, you must realize that the answer would be significant. It would set the stage for what was to be preached. Peter had just spent years under the instruction of the Lord Jesus Christ. He was not just a student but also a direct witness to what the Lord taught and what He did. Peter's answer to the question of the men in Jerusalem that day would have eternal implications so how he answered it was important. What Peter was doing was unlocking the kingdom of God to the people. Remember the Lord gave Peter the keys to the kingdom (Matthew 16:19) because he professed that Jesus is the Christ. On the day of Pentecost when the crowd asked men and brethren what must we do, he was unlocking the way to the kingdom of God by telling them what they need to do.

Then Peter said unto them, Repent, and be baptized every one of you in the name of Jesus Christ for the remission of sins, and ye shall receive the gift of the Holy Ghost. (Acts 2:38) This was not a suggestion nor was it something that was said on a whim. It was a command and if they want the gift of salvation that they need to repent, and be baptized in Jesus name for the remission of sins, and they shall receive the gift of the Holy Ghost. To belong to Christ and be a part of the church, this is what they must do. This is the Apostles doctrine! From the day of Pentecost throughout the Acts of the Apostles, this is how they taught.

> *1 Corinthians 15:1-4 Moreover, brethren, I declare unto you the gospel which I preached unto you, which also ye have received, and wherein ye stand; By which also ye are saved, if ye keep in memory what I preached unto you, unless ye have believed in vain. For I delivered unto you first of all that which I also received, how that Christ died for our sins according to the scriptures; And that he was buried, and that he rose again the third day according to the scriptures: (1 Corinthians 15:1-4)*

Paul told us in this passage exactly what the gospel is. He stated that he declares it, which he also preached, and we also received, and by which we stand.

He continued by saying that we also are saved by it if we keep in memory what was preached. He said that he delivers unto us what he received. This is what we must do. We must preach it as we received. No more and no less. Paul knew this and did exactly that. He said that the first thing he received was that Christ died for our sins according to the scriptures. He said that Christ was buried, and that He rose again the third day according to the scriptures. Paul taught that the gospel was the death, burial, and resurrection of Jesus Christ.

This passage is important because Paul was establishing what often gets missed. Many just concentrate on the death of Jesus. The death of Jesus is fundamental. It is what set the plan of salvation into motion. Without shedding His blood there would be no salvation but many believe by His blood and that's it. There is more to the Gospel than His death. Paul said it was the death, burial, and resurrection of Jesus Christ according to the scriptures so why did Paul put it that way? To understand this, it is also important to explain another common phrase that is derived from scripture.

Though he were a Son, yet learned he obedience by the things which he suffered; And being made perfect, he became the author of eternal salvation unto all them that obey him; (Hebrews 5:8-9) Jesus, through His obedience in the things that He suffered, became the author of salvation. He authored salvation through what He did through His obedience and if the full gospel of Jesus Christ is His death, burial, and resurrection then He authored salvation through death, burial, and resurrection. Paul stated that is the Gospel. In essence, it wasn't His death only that saved us but also His burial, and resurrection, by which He authored salvation. To receive salvation, we must obey Him. How does one obey the death, burial, and resurrection of Jesus Christ? Peter gave us that answer in Acts 2:38. We must repent, be baptized in Jesus name for the remission of sins, and be filled with the Holy Ghost.

When reading through New Testament writing, the Gospel is presented this way. Often people like to take pieces of the Bible and say this is how we're saved but that can't be done. To properly navigate through the Bible, one must know it is line upon line and precept upon precept (Isaiah 28). Sound doctrine is not based off of a single scripture but line upon line and precept upon precept. So, how do repentance, baptism, and being filled with the Holy Ghost obey Jesus's death, burial, and resurrection? Scripture gives us clues on how this is done.

Obeying the death of Jesus Christ is done through repentance. Repentance is more than just asking forgiveness for sins and asking for Jesus to be Lord of your life. Many bring people to this point and then say they are born again but being born again is more than this. Being born again is the entire command that given by Peter through repentance, baptism, and the infilling of the Holy Ghost. Jesus spoke specifically concerning the requirement to be born again.

> *Jesus answered and said unto him, Verily, verily, I say unto thee, Except a man be born again, he cannot see the kingdom of God. Nicodemus saith unto him, How can a man be born when he is old? can he enter the second time into his mother's womb, and be born? Jesus answered, Verily, verily, I say unto thee, Except a man be born of water and of the Spirit, he cannot enter into the kingdom of God. (John 3:3-5)*

Without question, people must be born again to enter the kingdom of God and that is why that term is used to express one's salvation. If you're born again you will enter the kingdom of God. The issue is not whether one must be born again, the issue is how does one get born again, which is what Nicodemus was asking when responding to Jesus about being born again. Jesus responded in a way that may surprise many and that is you must be born of the water and the Spirit. Many presume the water means a natural birth and in

68

John 3:6, Jesus speaks being born of man and Spirit but water there does not refer to the womb. A Strong's Concordance search will show that water refers to water that is of the earth whether in pools, rivers, oceans, etc. The reference there is not the water in the womb.

What Jesus said lines up with what Peter said in Acts 2:38. Being born again requires water baptism for the remission of sins and being filled with the Holy Ghost. The particulars of those will be discussed as this chapter progresses, but the point of explaining this now is to show that being born again is not complete when we "accept Jesus into our heart". The terms "accept Jesus in your heart" and "sinner's prayer" are never mentioned in the Bible yet the majority of Christian churches use these to indicate that a person is saved or born again, while ignoring Biblical doctrine.

If repentance is alone does not mean we are born again then what is it? The word, repent, means to change one's mind. In the relevance to salvation, it means to turn from one's life of sin unto a life after the Living God. Another way to say this is the sinner is dying to his former life and turning to a life after Jesus Christ. Just as Christ died for the sins of the world, repentance is the individual dying to one's self and living a new life in obedience to Jesus. To live this life after Christ is a constant dying to self. It is denying the desires of the flesh and of this world and seeking those things that are eternal and from God.

> *I protest by your rejoicing which I have in Christ Jesus our Lord, I die daily. If after the manner of men I have fought with beasts at Ephesus, what advantageth it me, if the dead rise not? let us eat and drink; for to morrow we die. Be not deceived: evil communications corrupt good manners. Awake to righteousness, and sin not; for some have not the knowledge of God: I speak this to your shame. (1 Corinthians 15:31-34)*

Paul was expressing that living after the Lord Jesus is a daily devotion and a daily putting down the flesh and refraining from sinful behavior. It is this idea of eternal salvation that is the focus of the Christian life and to attain that salvation means the Christian must deny his former life and embrace obedience to Christ and in that obedience comes freedom or new life. This is where repentance is continuous. While the Christian seeks to remain sin free, sometimes he fails. In confessing that failure before God, there is grace and forgiveness, if it is sought with contrition. This means with brokenness and sorrow, desiring to have this sin removed from your life. To express how living after Christ means denying the things of this world would mean putting the entire Bible into this book. The Lord expressed through His word that Christian life means being separate from this world.

> *Be ye not unequally yoked together with unbelievers: for what fellowship hath righteousness with unrighteousness? and what communion hath light with darkness? And what concord hath Christ with Belial? or what part hath he that believeth with an infidel? And what agreement hath the temple of God with idols? for ye are the temple of the living God; as God hath said, I will dwell in them, and walk in them; and I will be their God, and they shall be my people. Wherefore come out from among them, and be ye separate, saith the Lord, and touch not the unclean thing; and I will receive you, And will be a Father unto you, and ye shall be my sons and daughters, saith the Lord Almighty. (2 Corinthians 6:14-18)*

This is one of the many scriptures that discuss the need to live apart from the world. Of course, there is interaction with the world because the church still must preach to the world but this must be done without intertwining with the world. Fellowship must be with the saints of God and then reach out to the world when preaching the Gospel. That is what our witness is about but that's the extent of our interaction with the world. We are in the world, but we do not belong to this world. We belong to Jesus. Our fellowship now is with the saints who are of like precious faith that will encourage us to live after Christ. The world does the opposite.

What about grace? Doesn't God forgive when we sin? Yes He does, but grace can't be used as an excuse to sin. If the Christian is using grace as an excuse to sin, then he is not walking in repentance. He is still dead in his sin. Paul discussed this very point to the church in Rome.

> *Moreover the law entered, that the offence might abound. But where sin abounded, grace did much more abound: That as sin hath reigned unto death, even so might grace reign through righteousness unto eternal life by Jesus Christ our Lord. (Romans 5:20-21)*

In reading this alone, one could conclude that grace covers all but in the next chapter, Paul addresses the question. *What shall we say then? Shall we continue in sin, that grace may abound? God forbid. How shall we, that are dead to sin, live any longer therein? (Romans 6:1-2)* Paul asserted that grace is not a reason to sin nor is it used to soothe consciences when a person sins. Paul raised the question that if we are dead to sin, how can we live in it any longer? Then he explains a profound truth that shows how baptism is obedience to Jesus's burial.

> *Know ye not, that so many of us as were baptized into Jesus Christ were baptized into his death? Therefore we are buried with him by baptism into death: that like as Christ was raised up from the dead by the glory of the Father, even so we also should walk in newness*

of life. For if we have been planted together in
the likeness of his death, we shall be also in the
likeness of his resurrection: Knowing this, that
our old man is crucified with him, that the body
of sin might be destroyed, that henceforth we
should not serve sin. (Romans 6:3-6)

Those that are baptized into Jesus are buried with Him by baptism. This is concise explanation of why baptism is necessary. Scripture shows that baptism is done for the remission of sins (Acts 2:38). Now it shows that it is the believer's burial with Christ. It doesn't represent a burial nor is an outward sign of what's inside as many proclaim. Some proclaim that baptism isn't necessary and others proclaim that it is an outward sign of an inward work. Why can't we call it what the Bible says it is? It is our burial with Christ. This is how the believer obeys His burial. Through baptism, sins are remitted and washed away. This makes the Christian dead to sin so that from that point forward he should not be a servant to sin. Paul speaks of our burial with Christ in another place.

And ye are complete in him, which is the head
of all principality and power: In whom also ye
are circumcised with the circumcision made
without hands, in putting off the body of the sins
of the flesh by the circumcision of Christ:
Buried with him in baptism, wherein also ye are
risen with him through the faith of the operation
of God, who hath raised him from the dead. And
you, being dead in your sins and the
uncircumcision of your flesh, hath he quickened
together with him, having forgiven you all
trespasses. (Colossians 2:10-13)

Again, baptism is obedience to Christ's burial but there are other things this passage reveals concerning baptism. It is the circumcision of the flesh from the spirit. The flesh is worldly and sinful and baptism circumcises the body of sins. We're also told that baptism is not a work of man as many suppose which is why they suggest that it's not needed. They exclaim works don't save you, you are saved by faith, and therefore baptism is a work so it is not needed. Others baptize regularly but often as something that shows outwardly what is happening inwardly. Paul said baptism is a work of God and we have faith in the operation of God so that means being baptized we still operate under faith; therefore, it is necessary. Baptism is a work of faith and not a work of righteousness so in obedience to Christ's burial and for the remission of sins, baptism is required.

There are so many elements to the subject of baptism and the scriptures discuss this topic to length, yet there are preachers who state it's not needed or it is a choice if you want to do it. Yet, Peter commanded that the gentiles be baptized after they received the Holy Ghost.

> *And they of the circumcision which believed were astonished, as many as came with Peter, because that on the Gentiles also was poured out the gift of the Holy Ghost. For they heard them speak with tongues, and magnify God. Then answered Peter, Can any man forbid water, that these should not be baptized, which have received the Holy Ghost as well as we? And he commanded them to be baptized in the name of the Lord. Then prayed they him to tarry certain days. (Acts 10:45-48)*

I hope a couple thoughts are corrected with this passage. The first one being that it was not a choice to be baptized. Peter commanded that they be baptized. Just like at Pentecost when he instructed what they must do. There was no option, and the reason is that you have not obeyed the Gospel until you are baptized and filled with the Holy Ghost. You are buried with Christ at baptism.

This brings up the second point. Many say that it is not talking about water baptism, yet Peter asked them for water that the gentiles who received the Holy Ghost should be baptized. In another place Philip spoke to the Ethiopian Eunuch concerning Christ.

Then Philip opened his mouth, and began at the same scripture, and preached unto him Jesus. And as they went on their way, they came unto a certain water: and the eunuch said, See, here is water; what doth hinder me to be baptized? And Philip said, If thou believest with all thine heart, thou mayest. And he answered and said, I believe that Jesus Christ is the Son of God. And he commanded the chariot to stand still: and they went down both into the water, both Philip and the eunuch; and he baptized him. (Acts 8:35-38)

Again, baptism is referred to water baptism unless scripture differentiates, such as being baptized with the Holy Ghost and with fire (Matthew 3:11).

Thirdly, as seen from Philip to the Eunuch, Christ was preached, yet it does not specify what Philip said. It states he preached to him Jesus. The very next question from the Eunuch was here is water, what hinders me from being baptized? Reasonably, one must infer that in preaching Christ, baptism was also preached. It was a part of preaching the Gospel. Preachers today are using other methods of spreading the Gospel, which can't be found in scripture, yet these same preachers are exclaiming from the pulpit that baptism is not needed. The problem with that is, everywhere baptism is discussed in scripture shows it is needed. At some point, it becomes necessary to yield to scripture and not man's idea.

Fourthly, an element that is emphasized by Philip to the Eunuch is that you must believe. The Eunuch asked what prohibits from being baptized? Philip responded that if you believe, you could. The

74

confession that Jesus is the Son of God expressed his belief and he could be baptized in the water. This idea is conveyed in another place. The unfortunate thing is people use this scripture to say that all you have to do is believe and confess and you are saved.

> *That if thou shalt confess with thy mouth the Lord Jesus, and shalt believe in thine heart that God hath raised him from the dead, thou shalt be saved. For with the heart man believeth unto righteousness; and with the mouth confession is made unto salvation. For the scripture saith, Whosoever believeth on him shall not be ashamed. (Romans 10:9-11)*

Belief is a must. If you don't believe the Gospel then why would you obey it? Everything hinges on the point of belief. However, to state the believer needs to be baptized and filled with the Holy Ghost does not diminish the requirement to believe. Believing will move the believer to conversion and to obey the Gospel. Again, this is a consistent theme throughout the New Testament and Jesus made that exact statement. *And he said unto them, Go ye into all the world, and preach the gospel to every creature. He that believeth and is baptized shall be saved; but he that believeth not shall be damned. (Mark 16:15-16)* Jesus said he that believes and is baptized shall be saved.

To reiterate, this does not diminish the necessity to believe. Belief will compel to obedience of the Gospel. Faith produces action, as James said *Thou believest that there is one God; thou doest well: the devils also believe, and tremble. But wilt thou know, O vain man, that faith without works is dead? (James 2:19-20)* James emphasized that yes you must believe and you do well to do so but the devils also believe and they tremble. He said your belief; your faith is dead alone. Faith without works is dead.

It may be a shock that the Bible says that baptism is a requirement to be saved. Please understand, these are the Lord's words, not just a whimsical idea. This is what Jesus Christ said, who is the author of salvation (Hebrews 5:9). Romans 6 and Colossians 2 emphasize that it is obedience to the burial of Jesus Christ and there are other scriptures that discuss baptism with salvation.

> *Which sometime were disobedient, when once the longsuffering of God waited in the days of Noah, while the ark was a preparing, wherein few, that is, eight souls were saved by water. The like figure whereunto even baptism doth also now save us (not the putting away of the filth of the flesh, but the answer of a good conscience toward God,) by the resurrection of Jesus Christ: (1 Peter 3:20-21)*

What is Peter saying here? First, the plan of salvation is spoken throughout scripture. It is in the tabernacle plan given to Moses. It is in the expanse of creation from the world being washed in water during Noah's time and then with the heavens and the earth melting with a fervent heat and a new heaven and a new earth are created (2 Peter 3:10-13). So, it is no surprise that Peter refers to the flood during Noah's time as a baptism that saved eight souls by water and states that in the same way baptism saves us.

Baptism is not a ritual cleansing that puts away the filth of the flesh but it is deeper and gives a clean conscience toward God. Why? It is a spiritual cleansing where sins are washed away. *And now why tarriest thou? arise, and be baptized, and wash away thy sins, calling on the name of the Lord. (Acts 22:16)* Ananias said this to Paul a few days after Paul's encounter with the Lord on the road to Damascus. Ananias explained how Paul was to be a witness for the Lord Jesus Christ. The Lord blinded Paul during that encounter and sent Ananias to speak to him and tell him what he should do. The instruction was to be baptized and wash away his sins, calling on the name of the Lord. That answers the question about confession. Paul had to call on the name of the Lord and the Eunuch had to believe that Jesus Christ was the Son of God. These are confessions unto salvation and are accompanied by baptism.

So far we learned that repentance is obedience to the Lord's death and baptism is obedience to His burial. What is obedience to His resurrection? In following Peter's direction on the day of Pentecost, we must repent, be baptized in Jesus name for the remission of sins, and we shall receive the gift of the Holy Ghost. If repentance obeys His death and baptism obeys His burial, then the gift of the Holy Ghost obeys His resurrection. It should be no wonder because the Holy Ghost is life. *And if Christ be in you, the body is dead because of sin; but the Spirit is life because of righteousness. (Romans 8:10)*

Romans chapter 8 provides comprehensive insight into living a Christian life after the Spirit of God. It explains how we must have the Spirit and following the leading of the Spirit. In reality the Christian can't know God and follow God unless he is filled with the Holy Ghost. John the Baptist told us that aside from everything else Jesus came to do that He would fill us with the Holy Ghost and with fire. Jesus told us He would give life and give it more abundantly (John 10:10). This can only be accomplished through the power of the Holy Ghost. *But ye are not in the flesh, but in the Spirit, if the Spirit of God dwelleth in you. Now if any man hath not the Spirit of Christ, he is not his. (Romans 8:9)* To belong to Christ, having the Spirit of Christ is necessary. What does it mean to have the Holy Ghost? How does one get the Holy Ghost?

As with many doctrines, this is riddled in debate and misunderstanding and it doesn't have to be. There are those who believe that the moment you believe you have received the Spirit. There is significant scriptural evidence to suggest that is not true. We can start with the Roman church. Paul wrote his letters to existing churches. These were believers yet Paul addressed them with phrases like *"if the Spirit of God dwelleth in you"*.

77

Since he was speaking to a church of believers and he made that statement, then the assumption must be that some who believe didn't have the Spirit of God in them. This is made much clearer in the book of Acts when Paul came upon certain disciples.

> *And it came to pass, that, while Apollos was at Corinth, Paul having passed through the upper coasts came to Ephesus:and finding certain disciples, He said unto them, Have ye received the Holy Ghost since ye believed? And they said unto him, We have not so much as heard whether there be any Holy Ghost. And he said unto them, Unto what then were ye baptized? And they said, Unto John's baptism. Then said Paul, John verily baptized with the baptism of repentance, saying unto the people, that they should believe on him which should come after him, that is, on Christ Jesus. When they heard this, they were baptized in the name of the Lord Jesus. And when Paul had laid his hands upon them, the Holy Ghost came on them; and they spake with tongues, and prophesied. (Acts 19:1-6)*

This is clear evidence that receiving of the Holy Ghost is beyond when we believe. Paul asked them the question "Have ye received the Holy Ghost since ye believed?" If the Holy Ghost is received at belief, then Paul would not have had to ask that question. Then Paul asked them about their baptism because he knew something was wrong in their belief. They said they were baptized unto John so Paul preached Jesus and they were baptized into Christ, and Paul laid his hands on them and they received the Holy Ghost and Paul knew this because they spoke with tongues, which is the sign that the believer is filled with the Spirit. Yes, they prophesied also, but they spoke with tongues first.

*Now when the apostles which were at Jerusalem
heard that Samaria had received the word of
God, they sent unto them Peter and John: Who,
when they were come down, prayed for them,
that they might receive the Holy Ghost: (For as
yet he was fallen upon none of them: only they
were baptized in the name of the Lord Jesus.)
Then laid they their hands on them, and they
received the Holy Ghost. (Acts 8:14-17)*

Once again, we see believers who had not
received the Holy Ghost. They received the word and
were baptized in the name of Jesus but they had not
received the Holy Ghost. Peter and John had to be sent
to lay hands on them in order for them to be filled with
the Holy Ghost and once again there is visible evidence
of receiving the Holy because the very next verse
begins with *And when Simon saw that through laying
on of the apostles 'hands the Holy Ghost was given...
(Acts 8:18)* What did Simon witness when he saw they
were filled? It is the same sign they always looked for
and the same sign Peter was addressing on the day of
Pentecost - speaking in tongues.

*And they of the circumcision which believed
were astonished, as many as came with Peter,
because that on the Gentiles also was poured
out the gift of the Holy Ghost. For they heard
them speak with tongues, and magnify God.
(Acts 10:45-46)*

This is when the Holy Ghost fell on the Gentiles
and they knew they were filled because they heard
them speak with tongues, and magnify God. The
evidence is clear that the phenomenon associated with
being filled with the Holy Ghost is speaking in tongues.
It is the consistent pattern and God gave a sign by
which we can know we are filled, not just guess. The
reason is it is the Holy Ghost that changes us and by
which we truly commune with God. *For with*

stammering lips and another tongue will he speak to this people. To whom he said, This is the rest wherewith ye may cause the weary to rest; and this is the refreshing: yet they would not hear. (Isaiah 28:11-12) Speaking in tongues is our rest and our refreshing. It is also how God speaks to us and how we communicate with Him. Spiritual things are discerned spiritually and for the Christian that is by the Spirit of God. This is how God designed it and how the Apostle's taught it. Many in the church today believe this and are filled and they're lives are changed because of it.

Many also suffer today because they aren't filled with the Holy Ghost. They are in constant chaos because they aren't finding rest and refreshing through speaking to God with stammering lips and an unknown tongue. Also, many who have received the gift of the Holy Ghost are suffering because they aren't obeying Romans when Paul said, *For as many as are led by the Spirit of God, they are the sons of God. For ye have not received the spirit of bondage again to fear; but ye have received the Spirit of adoption, whereby we cry, Abba, Father. (Romans 8:14-15)* Upon receiving the Holy Ghost, we must also follow His leading. Then are we able to be called sons of God. You must let the Spirit of God change you to reflect God. All evidence seen of biblical conversion showed real change in the believer. This is why the Holy Ghost is given and why it is fundamental to being born again.

At this point, hopefully you see how Peter's command in Acts 2:38 is the way a soul obeys the Gospel of Jesus Christ. The obedience to the Gospel is wrapped up in the three elements in that passage. Repentance obeys Christ's death, baptism obeys His burial, and the gift of the Holy Ghost obeys His resurrection. The constant theme throughout the Bible reflects all of those elements and one must conclude to be born again, this is what we must do.

Why is this important when discussing the end times and the return of Christ? *And this gospel of the kingdom shall be preached in all the world for a witness unto all nations; and then shall the end come. (Matthew 24:14)* This is the Gospel we must preach and there are ministers around the world preaching it that way. Jesus said it must be preached and when the preaching of it witnesses to all nations, then the end shall come. The Gospel is constant and no matter what happens in the world, the church must preach it!

Chapter 6

The Last Days Church

Then shall they deliver you up to be afflicted, and shall kill you: and ye shall be hated of all nations for my name's sake. And then shall many be offended, and shall betray one another, and shall hate one another. And many false prophets shall rise, and shall deceive many. And because iniquity shall abound, the love of many shall wax cold. But he that shall endure unto the end, the same shall be saved. And this gospel of the kingdom shall be preached in all the world for a witness unto all nations; and then shall the end come. (Matthew 24:9-14)

Along with the preaching of the Gospel, there are taught certain expectations of the church. Jesus warned of false Christ's and false Messiahs. This is very important to remember because as you will see many will claim that the Lord has come and the Lord is here. They will reject the truth that is brought. I'm not speaking of the world's perception of the truth. I am speaking of the truth as the Bible teaches it, which is what this book is attempting to show. Because the world doesn't perceive Biblical truth, it will reject it either part or in its entirety. This is what will cause affliction among the believers.

Jesus said we must endure and in our endurance we shall be saved. If we fail to endure then we risk salvation. It's an absurd belief that the church will not go through tribulation. The early church did and in the modern day we see saints around the world being persecuted. There is a rise in anti-Christian sentiment and that will get worse. The name of Christ is hated, even in countries that pride themselves on freedom of religion. The politically correct (PC) culture has bred intolerance toward the name of Jesus Christ. This PC mindset dictates that everyone must compromise to prevent an individual or group from being offended by something. It says we must be tolerant of everyone's beliefs and that we all can co-exist in this world.

The problem is it requires compromise of beliefs, which is something a Christian can never do. Christians believe that Jesus Christ is the only way to salvation. The world would have us believe that there are multiple ways a person can be saved. It's not true. Through Jesus Christ comes salvation. There is no other way and if someone believes that there is another way, they are not Christian. It doesn't matter if they call themselves Christian, by professing that there are other ways to be saved means they aren't Christian.

Because Christians believe Jesus is the only way makes us fall under the category of "religious exclusiveness". This is a problem in the world's mind because to believe that goes against their agenda. They want to unite the world through religion and Christians will not unite under a banner that denies that Jesus is the only way to be saved. So, they say Christians are "intolerant". This is hypocrisy at its best. The people that push for tolerance of everyone's beliefs are not tolerant of those who believe in one way to salvation. They are the most intolerant individuals because they are putting into law that classifies those who hold to religious exclusiveness as terrorists.

It is typical of liberal ideology to say that you can believe what you want as long as you believe the same way they do. If you believe differently than how they believe, they will defame you and assassinate your character. They may not say this but this is what happens. They say everyone's beliefs are valid but if you don't support principles that go against your belief then they will try to force you to comply through the courts. Christian businesses are attacked for their stance against homosexuality. Military personnel are punished because they say the name of Jesus in their prayer. Atheists are trying to rid the name of Jesus Christ out of every bit of society. There is an attack on Christianity and the church is witnessing the seeds of tribulation already.

Seeds get watered and grow because the anti-Christian soil is fertile ground for that ideology to grow. It should be no surprise because throughout human history, the people of God were persecuted because we maintain that there is on One God and His name is Jesus. The church bows down to no other name than Jesus Christ and that puts us at odds with the world. It always has and it will until our Lord returns and then something strange happens.

> *That at the name of Jesus every knee should bow, of things in heaven, and things in earth, and things under the earth; And that every tongue should confess that Jesus Christ is Lord, to the glory of God the Father. (Philippians 2:10-11)*

The thing that people don't want to do is the thing they will do when the Lord returns. They shall bow down to Him and confess that Jesus Christ is Lord. No matter what a person believes now, they will confess that Jesus Christ is Lord when He comes back. There will be no atheist at that point in time.

We live in a day of choice. It is the dispensation of grace and God's grace is extended to us now. We make the choice to believe and to serve Him. Every day we wake up we have a choice to follow Him. The only problem with that is that God is not executing immediate judgment so we treat His grace carelessly. We mistake grace for absolution regardless of the intentions of our hearts. We feel free to sin with the belief that God's love will forgive our sin whether we repent or not. The day will come when God will judge sin and it won't be good for those that are judged according to their sin. Today is the day of choice and when you obey His Gospel, He will forgive you and wash away your sins. Then He will sanctify you by filling you with His Spirit and if following His leading, you will have eternal life.

85

To follow Christ is the greatest decision one can make in their entire life. It trumps everything else that we do because this is what God is after. He is after your soul but He is not just going to force His will on you. He doesn't work that way. We have to believe Him and chose His way. In choosing His way we become different. *Therefore if any man be in Christ, he is a new creature: old things are passed away; behold, all things are become new. (2 Corinthians 5:17)* Following Christ changes you. It changes your perception of the world. It changes your ambitions and prioritizes what is important in your life. These changes will put you at odds with the world that refuses to bow down to the One True God.

After we believe and obey His Gospel, then we must preach it. *And this gospel of the kingdom shall be preached in all the world for a witness unto all nations; and then shall the end come. (Matthew 24:14)* This means we must do so all the way until the end. The Great Commission has never ceased and no matter what is going on around us, we fulfill that commission until the Lord returns. That means when it is popular to preach it and in the face of persecution. We must follow the example of the early church. They faced affliction and persecution under the tyranny of the Roman Empire. Jesus prophesied that the end time church would face tribulation like never seen. The hatred of the name of Jesus Christ will be strong and the antichrist spirit will be dominant in the earth.

As the church, we must remember this is the will of God and there is purpose in everything. It won't change because the Bible says it will happen. We can't change it but we can turn our hearts to God and be strong in Him.

> *And such as do wickedly against the covenant shall he corrupt by flatteries: but the people that do know their God shall be strong, and do exploits. And they that understand among the people shall instruct many: yet they shall fall by*

*the sword, and by flame, by captivity, and by
spoil, many days. (Daniel 11:32-33)*

This passage is speaking of the time of the antichrist,
the man of sin, the son of perdition, or whatever term
you call him. So as this is the time of tribulation, there
is a noteworthy instruction concerning the church. They
that know their God shall be strong and do exploits and
they that have understanding among the people shall
instruct many. It's time to know God. Knowing God is
more than just believing that He exists. It is a
relationship with God that transforms the believer into a
son of God. This is only done through obedience to His
Gospel and the power of the Holy Ghost.

Scripture commands *"And be not conformed to
this world: but be ye transformed by the renewing of
your mind, that ye may prove what is that good, and
acceptable, and perfect, will of God." (Romans 12:2)*
Most people are conforming to this world. Even those
who profess Christianity are adopting the worldview on
many things. Long held Christian doctrine is being
compromised due to the pressure of modern day
agendas. The pressure from the world is causing the
church to change its principles to look like the world.
This is the wrong direction. We are not to conform to
this world but we are to be transformed by the renewing
of our mind. We are to walk as children of light and be
a city on a hill and to show the world the truths of
Christ, not fall prey to secular edicts and heresies.

These false doctrines will worsen as we see the
time of the antichrist draw near. Like the kings that
have gone before him, he will change laws to persecute
the church. These laws will be worldly ideals and come
against the righteous stand the church is supposed to be
maintaining. There is an ever-present evil in this world
that will seek to destroy any move of God of the time.
It is the battle the church must fight. The church the
tools to fight but it must make the decision to follow
God's will and not the ways of the world.

87

This is a day of cultural mindsets where anything goes. It is a day of people not wanting to be accountable for their actions. The political correctness and tolerance mentality has fooled people in believing that no judgment is allowed. They believe that God is love and He will forgive anything. They not only believe He will but it is almost expected that He must, and that is where the slippery slope begins. To think that the Lord is required to do anything is an arrogant belief. God does because He is faithful and He is love, but to expect forgiveness without repentance is a gross error. Remember, repentance is not only asking forgiveness (with contrition that is) but it also means turning from your sinful lifestyle to a life pleasing unto God. To continue in sin does not please God.

God is particular about His word. Everything that God says is crafted carefully and meticulously because in God's view the word is powerful. It is forever settled in heaven (Psalms 119:89) and why man must live by every word that proceeds from the mouth of the Lord (Matthew 4:4, Luke 4:4). It is true (Psalms 119:160) and serves as a light unto our paths and a lamp unto our feet (Psalms 119:105). It is to be obeyed and not changed but there are many in the world that would like to change it. There are many false prophets that seek to diminish the word of God and say it doesn't mean what it says.

Jeremiah serves as a perfect illustration of this. Jeremiah chapters 27 and 28 shows how Jeremiah the prophet of God went into Zedekiah, king of Judah and prophesied how it is the will of God that Babylon will lay siege to Jerusalem and that Judah must surrender and go into captivity in Babylon. He prophesied that God would bless this and break the yoke of Babylon if Judah will surrender. No king wants to hear the words surrender and as sure as there are prophets of God there are also false prophets and Hananiah was such a prophet. He showed his false prophecy by breaking the yoke that Jeremiah carried in and Hananiah made the following false prophecy. *And Hananiah spake in the*

presence of all the people, saying, Thus saith the Lord;
Even so will I break the yoke of Nebuchadnezzar king
of Babylon from the neck of all nations within the space
of two full years. And the prophet Jeremiah went his
way. (Jeremiah 28:11)

Hananiah gave the word that was popular and what the king wanted to hear. Jeremiah spoke truth and it was unpopular and they persecuted him for speaking the truth. Just because something is popular doesn't make it the truth. The world today is very near sighted in many things. They fall for the flavor of the day and fail to realize the detrimental effects of the lies they perpetuate. The problem with false prophecy is that it will not happen and the decision that is made in that moment could cause damage for generations to come. Many false prophets are speaking lies that are the popular view and those that hold to Biblical truth are being persecuted. False prophets preach false doctrine and they ridicule the truth and those that preach it.

In present times the church faces many false teachings. They are wrapped in buzzwords such as "progress" and "moving forward". There is a belief that the old ways are out of date and need to catch up with the times. People try to convince us that Biblical principle is no longer relevant in the modern world. Some even have said that the Bible needs to catch up with today. I would expect this from people outside the church. My worry is about those who profess Christianity and make these statements or allow abominable practices to enter into the church. They ignore scripture to follow evil practices and fail to realize the sinful snare they are caught in. When you can justify sinful behavior, you are on a slippery slope.

The church faces compromising behavior that has been in work for some time but has manifested rapidly in recent years. The storm didn't just come out of nowhere. It has been brewing as evildoers have chipped away at the truth to the point where people don't even know what truth is anymore. Sinful practices in the church have been excused instead of corrected. Preachers have become more concerned with filling pews rather than filling heaven. Popularity has won over truth because it is easier to follow a preacher whose preaching will not bring conviction about the wrong you do in your life. It is no wonder that divorce rates in the church have skyrocketed and adultery and homosexuality is running rampant in the church, let alone in the world. When a church can reach the point to say God accepts that homosexual lifestyle, it has gone over the cliff.

Before feathers get ruffled, let me assure you that homosexuality is forgivable, just like any other sin, but it is not acceptable to God, just like any other sin. Therefore, the church should not accept it and if it does, that is a false church. We have to realize that homosexuality is a sin and it must be repented of and that means the homosexual must stop committing the act and come out of it. I have heard countless justifications for this sin ranging from they are born that way to God is love, therefore, He would honor the love between two people no matter who they are. I've even heard people say that there are only a few passages that speak against homosexuality and there are many that speak against divorce, yet we accept divorce and not homosexuality.

There are some things wrong with this thinking. The "few" passages that speak against homosexuality make them irrelevant? *All scripture is given by inspiration of God, and is profitable for doctrine, for reproof, for correction, for instruction in righteousness: (2 Timothy 3:16)* The few passages that speak against homosexuality still show that God is against it. There is never any favorable end for those who practice this lifestyle. Secondly, no sin is acceptable to God so things like divorce and remarriage, adultery, murder, stealing, drunkenness (which includes drugs), fornication, and anything God says is sin, is sin! The church should not accept sin. One sin is not any more justifiable than another sin and it all requires repentance.

That being said, it is important to note that the enemy of our souls has been wearing down the righteousness of humanity from the beginning of time. God makes a command and the devil is there to deceive man from following God's commands. In the case of homosexuality, it is an advance in the degradation of righteousness throughout the world. The issue before us is the definition of marriage, which already shown is given by God as between one man and one woman. Anything outside of God's definition of marriage is perversion so that includes a laundry list of sins. They are adultery (to include divorce and remarriage), fornication (to include sexual relationships without being married), whoredom (prostitution), self-gratification, and homosexuality (to include any variant such as bi-sexual, lesbianism, and transgender).

Marriage is really what is under attack here. Marriage is a covenant sanctified by God. It is a covenant between husband and wife and together they form a covenant with God that states some form of the phrase "until death do us part". So when marriage is diminished to nothing more than a civil legality, then it loses the sanctity that God puts on it and this will lead to sin. As a church, we must safeguard the sanctity and holiness of marriage and understand the covenant that is created when one enters into marriage. Equally, if we are going to make a stand against the sin of homosexuality, we must also make a stand against divorce and remarriage, adultery, sex before marriage, and any other sin that defies the sanctity of marriage.

People say that as long as they are not being bothered then anyone can live or believe what they want. They ignore sinful lifestyles as long as they aren't impacted by it. This is a deception that can be detrimental. *Who knowing the judgment of God, that they which commit such things are worthy of death, not only do the same, but have pleasure in them that do them. (Romans 1:32)* There is judgment for sin and God will judge those who commit the sin and those that have pleasure in them that do. The word pleasure here means to agree with or consent to. It also means to applaud and approve.

Currently, we are witnessing an approval and applauding of sinful behavior. Lifestyles we once knew were sinful are now being applauded as progressive and equal. One can understand this from those in the world, although they will be judged for their behavior, but for those of the faith it is deplorable to be accepting of such lifestyles. The judgment will be the same as if to commit the sin yourself. The world will do what the world will do but the church cannot and must not endorse lewdness and sinful practices. Of such are false doctrines and false prophets. Remember, the Bible warns vehemently concerning false apostles and false prophets. It warns of false teachings and doctrines of devils. Sin is still sin in the eyes of God and as the body of Christ; we must not be convinced that sin is acceptable.

The direction the church is headed is a wayward road. It is not the path of light. The church needs to do some self-examination and correct itself through the power of the Spirit of God and the Word of God. We need to return to Biblical Christianity so we can be an example for the world to follow.

> *Be ye not unequally yoked together with unbelievers: for what fellowship hath righteousness with unrighteousness? and what communion hath light with darkness? And what concord hath Christ with Belial? or what part hath he that believeth with an infidel? And what agreement hath the temple of God with idols? for ye are the temple of the living God; as God hath said, I will dwell in them, and walk in them; and I will be their God, and they shall be my people. Wherefore come out from among them, and be ye separate, saith the Lord, and touch not the unclean thing; and I will receive you, And will be a Father unto you, and ye shall*

be my sons and daughters, saith the Lord
Almighty. (2 Corinthians 6:14-18)

This passage clearly directs us to be separate from the
world and to come out from them. This doesn't mean
that we have no contact with the world or else we
wouldn't be able to witness to them but the church
can't look like the world. The church must separate
itself from communion and fellowship with the world.
Our communion and fellowship needs to be with
brothers and sisters in Christ and with the Lord
Himself.

> *Ye are the light of the world. A city that is set on*
> *an hill cannot be hid. Neither do men light a*
> *candle, and put it under a bushel, but on a*
> *candlestick; and it giveth light unto all that are*
> *in the house. Let your light so shine before men,*
> *that they may see your good works, and glorify*
> *your Father which is in heaven. (Matthew 5:14-*
> *16)*

Jesus told us that we are to be lights and we are
to let our lights shine. Today the church is hiding their
light under a bushel. There are sinful practices that we
know are not right, yet we sit back and say nothing.
Billions of people in this world are on a path to hell and
the church remains silent on how they can be saved.
The pressure of the world and the plan of Satan is
designed to silence the church so the light of truth
remains hidden. Jesus gave us the permission to light
this world with His light. They see our good works and
they give glory to God.

The problem is the church has lost its power, or
more accurately, the church is not utilizing the power
that was given. This is because of some of the previous
issues discussed such as apostasy and a failure to
adhere to the apostle's doctrine. The church is not
following the principles on which it was founded. Jesus
Christ came to give His followers power over sin and

spiritual darkness, yet many don't realize what that power is. Jesus also made that clear to us as well.

> *But ye shall receive power, after that the Holy Ghost is come upon you: and ye shall be witnesses unto me both in Jerusalem, and in all Judaea, and in Samaria, and unto the uttermost part of the earth. (Acts 1:8)*

The Spirit of God poured out on His believers is the power but the church today is not walking in that power. As a pastor, I have dealt with people whose lives are simply ones of total defeat. They have a spirit that has been totally trampled upon and beat up and you can see it in their faces.

Some came to us not filled with the Holy Ghost and others were never taught that they have the power through the Holy Ghost to overcome. Some have been serving in a church for twenty years or more and still did not know how to have power over the enemy of our souls and over temptations and sin. I recall a woman when I served in a church years ago who was struggling with her cigarette addiction. She wanted to give them up but lacked the power to do so and she brought it to the altar to receive prayer. The prayer team (of which I was a part) gathered around and took the pack of cigarettes and told her all she needs to do is stomp on them and make a commitment to God and she would be free from them. As we were praying the Lord revealed to me she needs the Holy Ghost to which I said she needs the Holy Ghost, yet they would not pray for her to receive the baptism of the Holy Ghost. They were caught up in the emotion of the moment telling her this is what you can do but she had no power to do it; she needed the power of God in her to overcome her addiction.

It is no wonder the church is dealing with the issues of today within itself. It is one thing to deal with the issues of the world around us but to have the same worldly issues in the church means that there is no power or conviction by the Spirit of God. You see, with the Holy Ghost also comes conviction when we go down roads we shouldn't. The Spirit convicts us on matters of truth so we don't stray from it. That's how He leads us to all truth. The power of the Holy Ghost in us doesn't just let us read a passage or hear a message and then expect us to walk in obedience to it, rather He leads us in how we can walk in obedience to it. He also shows us whether the understanding of the passage or the hearing of the message is truth or a twisting of the truth.

> *But ye have an unction from the Holy One, and ye know all things. I have not written unto you because ye know not the truth, but because ye know it, and that no lie is of the truth. (1 John 2:20-21)*

Unction here means anointing and when a believer is under the anointing, there is something inside that compels to follow after Christ. It can't be explained in mere words but it is a nudging inside that tells us that this is something that must be done. It just won't leave you alone and it is something that you know. This is the voice of the Lord and you can know it and you must know it, else the church will fail. The Lord Jesus told us that will not happen (Matthew 16:18) but we must be listening for the Lord and seeking the Unction from the Holy One. This is the only way we will know direction and righteousness.

This comes with a word of warning that many just ignore but to listen to the Spirit of God will put you at odds with the way of the world. Those who hear His voice won't do what the word does. They won't follow its sin and they will speak against it. This is what will cause persecution because the church will not obey the evil of the world. The church will obey God and it is because of the Unction of the Holy One. Consequently, this will lead to great tribulation. The persecution against the church has already begun but it's only the beginning, and to be strong in these times and to know what to do, we must learn the voice of the Lord.

Chapter 7

The Day of the Lord

The Day of the Lord

*But, beloved, be not ignorant of this one thing,
that one day is with the Lord as a thousand
years, and a thousand years as one day. The
Lord is not slack concerning his promise, as
some men count slackness; but is longsuffering
to us- ward, not willing that any should perish,
but that all should come to repentance. But the
day of the Lord will come as a thief in the night;
in the which the heavens shall pass away with a
great noise, and the elements shall melt with
fervent heat, the earth also and the works that
are therein shall be burned up. Seeing then that
all these things shall be dissolved, what manner
of persons ought ye to be in all holy
conversation and godliness, Looking for and
hasting unto the coming of the day of God,
wherein the heavens being on fire shall be
dissolved, and the elements shall melt with
fervent heat? Nevertheless we, according to his
promise, look for new heavens and a new earth,
wherein dwelleth righteousness. Wherefore,
beloved, seeing that ye look for such things, be
diligent that ye may be found of him in peace,
without spot, and blameless. (2 Peter 3:8-14)*

The day of the Lord is an anticipated event to
those who believe. It is the day the church longs for,
where the Lord sets everything right. Scripture tells us
we are to look for the day with anticipation. People
grow impatient in the waiting and some will question
and even mock those who believe in the Lord's return
and His timing. The Apostle Peter said not to be
ignorant concerning this. He said that God is not slack
in His promises. The reason God is waiting is because
of His patience and longsuffering. God is not willing
that any should perish and that all should come to
repentance so His waiting is for us. God is extending
His grace by waiting so that people get things right.

Peter also explained to us that the day would take the world as a thief. It will come in an hour where the world won't expect it and where people won't be looking for it but we are instructed to look for it. The church is to look for His return with haste and readying ourselves for His return. The key is to be looking for it so we don't miss it. If we are to look for it then there are signs that precede it to which we are seeing come to pass. In light of all happening in the world and how evil days are upon, scripture gives some important counsel on how to handle it.

> *For if we believe that Jesus died and rose again, even so them also which sleep in Jesus will God bring with him. For this we say unto you by the word of the Lord, that we which are alive and remain unto the coming of the Lord shall not prevent them which are asleep. For the Lord himself shall descend from heaven with a shout, with the voice of the archangel, and with the trump of God: and the dead in Christ shall rise first: Then we which are alive and remain shall be caught up together with them in the clouds, to meet the Lord in the air: and so shall we ever be with the Lord. Wherefore comfort one another with these words. (1 Thessalonians 4:14-18)*

We are told to comfort one another with these words. The words that those in Christ will see each other again when He returns and receives them unto Himself. Those that have gone on in the faith will rise and those who are alive and remain will ascend to meet them in the air. This is how it will happen and this is what the church will look for. Jesus gave a prophesy of false Christ's and false prophets who will say they are Him and how they will say He is in the desert or in the secret chamber (Matthew 24:26-28). Jesus said how He would come back and that is with lightning from east to west. He will descend from heaven with trumpets and lightning, not in secret. Those that say they've seen Him are false and not to be listened to. Matthew 24 also gives a clue when this will happen.

> *Immediately after the tribulation of those days shall the sun be darkened, and the moon shall not give her light, and the stars shall fall from heaven, and the powers of the heavens shall be shaken: And then shall appear the sign of the Son of man in heaven: and then shall all the tribes of the earth mourn, and they shall see the Son of man coming in the clouds of heaven with power and great glory. And he shall send his angels with a great sound of a trumpet, and they shall gather together his elect from the four winds, from one end of heaven to the other. (Matthew 24:29-31)*

Remember, these are the words of Jesus Christ. Matthew 24 is His chronology of end time events. There is no greater source of how the end time will play out than our Lord and God, Jesus Christ. He clearly states that His return occurs immediately after the tribulation of those days. As this passage describes it will be an event that is seen. It is not something that happens in secret. There is a major belief surrounding this event is that the church suddenly vanishes and no one will know where it went. Jesus did not describe it this way. He said there will be signs in the sky and the powers of heaven will shake and then we shall see Him. Look at what it says, "all the tribes of the earth shall mourn, and they shall see the Son of man coming in the clouds of heaven with power and great glory". Everyone will see this event. It will not be a silent affair. A trumpet will sound (the last trump) and He will send His angels to gather His elect from the four corners of the earth.

This description differs greatly from the common view that is being taught. This and other passages, which we will look at, indicate an event that is not secret, but for the world to see. He came the first time as the Lamb of God to take a way the sins of the world and He came into this world quietly (except for a proclamation to the shepherds on the night He was born). The second time He comes to this world is not in secret but for all people everywhere who will see Him. Where does this idea of secrecy come from?

For yourselves know perfectly that the day of the Lord so cometh as a thief in the night. (1 Thessalonians 5:2) Using this passage often cites the view that Christ's return is something that is imminent and secret. I often here "He shall come as a thief" or "no one knows the hour or the day" (Matthew 24:36, Matthew 25:13, Mark 13:32). Mark's passage states not even the Son knows, only the Father. These passages give an idea that His return can happen at any moment because He comes as a thief and we can't know the hour or the day. Paul states that the day of the Lord comes as a thief but look at what he says immediately after.

> *For when they shall say, Peace and safety; then sudden destruction cometh upon them, as travail upon a woman with child; and they shall not escape. But ye, brethren, are not in darkness, that that day should overtake you as a thief. Ye are all the children of light, and the children of the day: we are not of the night, nor of darkness. (1 Thessalonians 5:3-5)*

Paul gives powerful insight concerning the church and our Lord's return. He says yes the Lord will come as a thief but then he says that the church is not in darkness that the day should overtake us as a thief. Jesus returns as a thief to those who are in darkness but those that are following Him and looking for Him, that day won't take as a thief. Paul continues by saying *Therefore let us not sleep, as do others; but let us watch and be sober (1 Thessalonians 5:6)*. We are to watch and remain sober so we can discern the signs and the times and to ensure when He comes, we will go to be with Him. Paul's second letter to Thessalonica helps us to understand this matter better.

> *Now we beseech you, brethren, by the coming of our Lord Jesus Christ, and by our gathering together unto him, That ye be not soon shaken in mind, or be troubled, neither by spirit, nor by word, nor by letter as from us, as that the day of Christ is at hand. Let no man deceive you by any means: for that day shall not come, except there come a falling away first, and that man of sin be revealed, the son of perdition; Who opposeth and exalteth himself above all that is called God, or that is worshipped; so that he as God sitteth in the temple of God, shewing himself that he is God. (2 Thessalonians 2:1-4)*

This passage agrees with what Jesus told us in Matthew 24. Jesus said when we see the abomination of desolation (vs. 15), then shall there be great tribulation (vs. 21), and immediately after the tribulation of those days shall the Son of man return to gather the elect (vs. 29-31). This passage in 2 Thessalonians is dealing with the return of our Lord Jesus Christ. It starts off by discussing the coming of our Lord and our gathering unto Him. Paul comforts by saying we should not be soon shaken in mind by word or by letter as though the day of Christ is at hand. Paul dealt with this same issue in his day because they thought as many think today it will happen at any moment and he had to address it. Make no mistake; I am not implying that His return is not near. The signs of the times show we are in the season of His return but as Paul stated there is something we look for.

He continues by saying, "Let no man deceive you". Paul was telling us that talk of an immediate rapture is deception. He follows by giving a sign that must precede the Lord's return. He said the day of the Lord wouldn't happen until there is a falling away first and a man stands in the temple of God, proclaiming to be God. Paul says this man is the man of sin, the son of perdition, who opposes and exalts himself above all that is called God. This man of sin and son of perdition is whom we call Antichrist. What Paul is describing here is the abomination of desolation, which Jesus said we see before great tribulation and His return. *When ye therefore shall see the abomination of desolation, spoken of by Daniel the prophet, stand in the holy place, (whoso readeth, let him understand). (Matthew 24:15)* Jesus said the abomination of desolation would happen in the holy place. Paul said this man who opposes and exalts himself above all that is God happens in the temple of God, which is the holy place. Paul reiterated what Jesus said and that is the day of the Lord wouldn't happen until that event happens.

Jesus also said Daniel the Prophet spoke of this abomination of desolation, so what did Daniel say? This was discussed under chapter 2 "The Great Tribulation". Daniel said the abomination of desolation would happen in the midst of the week. Of that final seven years, the abomination of desolation happens half way through. According to Daniel, the confirmation of the covenant (peace agreement) will begin the final seven-year period. At the midpoint the abomination of desolation will be placed marking 3 ½ years of tribulation, and Jesus said immediately after the tribulation of those days, He will return to gather His elect. Paul gives the description of the abomination of desolation and agreed with the Lord and Paul state that it is something we need to be looking for.

Some would argue that this is for the Jews since Jesus spoke concerning those in Judea (known as the West Bank today). While that may be true, we have to remember Paul was speaking to the church which was a church in Macedonia, of Greek majority. From this we can draw that the same message applies to both Jew and the church. Those in Judea are impacted by great tribulation first, but it will filter to the rest of the world and will include the church. The mark of the beast in

103

Revelation 13 is how the world government system is designed so that those who do not comply with its edicts are persecuted and easily identifiable. The great tribulation will be a complete reliance on God and a renouncing of this world government system. We are seeing the seeds of persecution against the church in this world already. Those that endure tribulation will receive a wonderful reward.

> *And I saw thrones, and they sat upon them, and judgment was given unto them: and I saw the souls of them that were beheaded for the witness of Jesus, and for the word of God, and which had not worshipped the beast, neither his image, neither had received his mark upon their foreheads, or in their hands; and they lived and reigned with Christ a thousand years. But the rest of the dead lived not again until the thousand years were finished. This is the first resurrection. Blessed and holy is he that hath part in the first resurrection: on such the second death hath no power, but they shall be priests of God and of Christ, and shall reign with him a thousand years. (Revelation 20:4-6)*

We know persecution has happened throughout the ages and this reward certainly applies to those who stood on His word from the very beginning until the end. This scripture highlights those that come out of tribulation and did not bow down to the beast and his system, even though they were beheaded or who denied the mark of the beast. Notice what it says. They will partake of the first resurrection. This is the first resurrection which occurs after tribulation, not before. The second resurrection is the second death which occurs after the thousand-year reign of Christ when He wraps up all things and creates all things new. There is a resurrection unto life and a resurrection unto death. Revelation chapter 14 shows this in two harvests.

And I looked, and behold a white cloud, and upon the cloud one sat like unto the Son of man, having on his head a golden crown, and in his hand a sharp sickle. And another angel came out of the temple, crying with a loud voice to him that sat on the cloud, Thrust in thy sickle, and reap: for the time is come for thee to reap; for the harvest of the earth is ripe. And he that sat on the cloud thrust in his sickle on the earth; and the earth was reaped. And another angel came out of the temple which is in heaven, he also having a sharp sickle. And another angel came out from the altar, which had power over fire; and cried with a loud cry to him that had the sharp sickle, saying, Thrust in thy sharp sickle, and gather the clusters of the vine of the earth; for her grapes are fully ripe. And the angel thrust in his sickle into the earth, and gathered the vine of the earth, and cast it into the great winepress of the wrath of God. And the winepress was trodden without the city, and blood came out of the winepress, even unto the horse bridles, by the space of a thousand and six hundred furlongs. (Revelation 14:14-20)

John was shown a glimpse of two harvests from the earth. The first harvest was the reaping of the saints because the angel spoke to the Lord stating to thrust in His sickle and reap the harvest. This is the gathering of the elect. The second angel was instructed by another to thrust in his sickle and gather the clusters of the vine of the earth. This harvest is the wicked of the earth that would be thrown into the winepress of God's wrath. This shows two harvests that agree with Revelation 20 that shows the first resurrection and the second death. The first harvest is unto life, the second unto death. This should answer the question of two harvests, as some believe that there is the rapture that will harvest the elect from the earth and then a second harvest at the end of tribulation that will gather those that believed during the tribulation, but scripture doesn't support that belief. Revelation 20:5 states that the first resurrection happens after tribulation. This agrees with Jesus in Matthew 24:29 and with Paul in 2 Thessalonians 2:3-4.

The sounding of the seven trumpets also reinforces that the gathering of the elect happens after the tribulation. In fact, the tribulation occurs between the sounding of the sixth and seventh trumpets. The sixth trumpet sounds in Revelation 9:13 and warns of a war that will kill two-thirds of mankind. After the description of this war John is given a little book to eat that would taste sweet in his mouth bur make his belly bitter and he was told that he must prophesy again to many people, nations, and tongues (Revelation 10:10). Then John begins to prophesy about the temple and the outer court being trampled under foot for forty-two months (Revelation 11: 1-2). John also speaks of the two witnesses and their testimony, which is for 1,260 days (Revelation 11:3-14). This is also the time of great tribulation and if you calculate forty-two months and 1,260 days you arrive at 3 ½ years, which is the length of the great tribulation.

Revelation 11:15 starts by the sounding of the seventh trumpet, which is the gathering of the elect and the day of the Lord. Once again, this occurs after the tribulation coinciding with the other scriptures discussed previously. After reading these passages one must concede that rapture follows the tribulation, as it is consistent throughout scripture from the words of Christ through Paul and in the Revelation given to John. Daniel also prophesies of this in Daniel chapter 7.

> *I beheld, and the same horn made war with the saints, and prevailed against them; Until the Ancient of days came, and judgment was given to the saints of the most High; and the time came that the saints possessed the kingdom. (Daniel 7:21-22)*

The horn here is the antichrist. This horn makes war against the saints until the Ancient of days comes, and gives judgment to the saints, and along with Him, we possess the kingdom. What a glorious promise but Daniel shows that there will be trouble for the saints of God prior to the Lord's return and agreeing with what we have read concerning His timing. Now the question is, what happens under the seventh trumpet? Let's begin with Paul's account.

> *Behold, I shew you a mystery; We shall not all sleep, but we shall all be changed, In a moment, in the twinkling of an eye, at the last trump: for the trumpet shall sound, and the dead shall be raised incorruptible, and we shall be changed. For this corruptible must put on incorruption, and this mortal must put on immortality. So when this corruptible shall have put on incorruption, and this mortal shall have put on immortality, then shall be brought to pass the saying that is written, Death is swallowed up in victory. O death, where is thy sting? O grave, where is thy victory? The sting of death is sin; and the strength of sin is the law. But thanks be to God, which giveth us the victory through our Lord Jesus Christ. (1 Corinthians 15:51-57)*

Supporters of the imminent return doctrine also use this scripture to state that it can happen at any moment and in the twinkling of an eye but what does Paul say is really happening here? He states twice in the first few lines that we shall be changed. When the trumpet sounds the dead will rise and we shall be changed. Our corruptible flesh will put on incorruption. Our mortality will put on immortality. In other words, what happens in a moment and in the twinkling of an eye is we receive our glorified bodies. It doesn't state that the church will suddenly disappear into the sky to be with our Lord. It merely states that we will be changed from our corruptible flesh to a glorified body

107

much like that of Jesus Christ when He resurrected from the grave.

Remember, they saw Him, but they saw Him in His glorified state and as scripture shows this was for forty days until He ascended to heaven when they watched Him be caught up (Acts 1:9). This seems to indicate the church will be seen as we are caught up. Even the two witnesses are watched as their bodies are resurrected and caught up (Revelation 11: 12). The two witnesses resurrection is at the timing of the seventh trumpet so there is a consistent pattern of people observing the catching up of the righteous. It's not going to be a quiet affair. Paul gives another view of what happens during this event.

> *For this we say unto you by the word of the Lord, that we which are alive and remain unto the coming of the Lord shall not prevent them which are asleep. For the Lord himself shall descend from heaven with a shout, with the voice of the archangel, and with the trump of God: and the dead in Christ shall rise first: Then we which are alive and remain shall be caught up together with them in the clouds, to meet the Lord in the air: and so shall we ever be with the Lord. Wherefore comfort one another with these words. (1 Thessalonians 4:15-18)*

The Lord shall descend from heaven with a shout, the voice of the archangel, and with the trump of God. When you think about all of these things, it is a proclamation. It is a signal as to what is happening. The Lord is letting the world know that He has come for His bride. Those that are dead will rise first and those who are alive will be caught up to meet with them in the air, and we will forever be with the Lord. This is the event of events and one that we wait for with anticipation but it is at the last trumpet and there are events that happen prior to sounding of the last trumpet. As you read through the seven trumpets of Revelation, you see how these events unfold. If the rapture happens at the last trumpet that means the church is here through the first six trumpets. Let's take a look at Revelation's account of the seventh trumpet.

> *And the seventh angel sounded; and there were great voices in heaven, saying, The kingdoms of this world are become the kingdoms of our Lord, and of his Christ; and he shall reign for ever and ever. And the four and twenty elders, which sat before God on their seats, fell upon their faces, and worshipped God, Saying, We give thee thanks, O Lord God Almighty, which art, and wast, and art to come; because thou hast taken to thee thy great power, and hast reigned. And the nations were angry, and thy wrath is come, and the time of the dead, that they should be judged, and that thou shouldest give reward unto thy servants the prophets, and to the saints, and them that fear thy name, small and great; and shouldest destroy them which destroy the earth. And the temple of God was opened in heaven, and there was seen in his temple the ark of his testament: and there were lightnings, and voices, and thunderings, and an earthquake, and great hail. (Revelation 11:15-19)*

The seventh trumpet ushers in the Kingdom of God. After gathering His saints from the world, Jesus takes dominion away from the nations of the world and He establishes His Kingdom and will rule at first for one thousand years and after the creation of a new heaven and a new earth, forever. The seventh trumpet also ushers in a time of judgment and for those who rejected His salvation and persecuted His people, a time of His wrath. In the book of Revelation, the wrath of God can be seen beginning in chapter 16. *And I heard a great voice out of the temple saying to the seven angels,*

Go your ways, and pour out the vials of the wrath of
God upon the earth. (Revelation 16:1)

What follows are the vials being poured out on
those that took the mark of the beast and then on the
unbelievers through various judgments. This will look
much like the plagues that were poured out on Egypt
when Pharaoh rejected God's command through Moses
to "let my people go". People today are taking a
combative approach to wipe out anything that has to do
with God and His Christ. If you read through the vials
of God's wrath, you will find that men still didn't
repent rather they cursed the Living God for the
plagues that fell.

God is good and merciful, but He is also
righteous and true. The world has come to the point of
outright mockery and denial of His existence. They fail
to reach out to the hand of grace that is currently
extended through salvation in Jesus Christ. They reject
anything that has to do with Him because "nobody is
going to tell them what to do". In rebellion they
blaspheme Him and through their arrogance, they
believe that nothing will happen to them. They
persecute God's people and think they are doing the
world a service by getting rid of these "fanatics". At the
seventh trumpet, they will find out that this does not
please God and there is no one to blame. They fail to
heed the warning from God's word and from His
church and it will catch up to them. Remember, every
knee shall bow and every tongue confesses that Jesus
Christ is Lord (Philippians 2:10-11). If you don't do it
now you will do it then.

Now that we know how God will deal with the
ungodly, what does His return bring for the church?
We've already established that Jesus will set up His
Kingdom and the church will be a part of His rule. We
know the church will be caught up to meet with Him in
the air but what happens after?

> *And I heard as it were the voice of a great*
> *multitude, and as the voice of many waters, and*

as the voice of mighty thunderings, saying,
Alleluia: for the Lord God omnipotent reigneth.
Let us be glad and rejoice, and give honour to
him: for the marriage of the Lamb is come, and
his wife hath made herself ready. And to her
was granted that she should be arrayed in fine
linen, clean and white: for the fine linen is the
righteousness of saints. And he saith unto me,
Write, Blessed are they which are called unto
the marriage supper of the Lamb. And he saith
unto me, These are the true sayings of God. And
I fell at his feet to worship him. And he said
unto me, See thou do it not: I am thy
fellowservant, and of thy brethren that have the
testimony of Jesus: worship God: for the
testimony of Jesus is the spirit of prophecy. And
I saw heaven opened, and behold a white horse;
and he that sat upon him was called Faithful
and True, and in righteousness he doth judge
and make war. His eyes were as a flame of fire,
and on his head were many crowns; and he had
a name written, that no man knew, but he
himself. And he was clothed with a vesture
dipped in blood: and his name is called The
Word of God. And the armies which were in
heaven followed him upon white horses, clothed
in fine linen, white and clean. And out of his
mouth goeth a sharp sword, that with it he
should smite the nations: and he shall rule them
with a rod of iron: and he treadeth the
winepress of the fierceness and wrath of
Almighty God. And he hath on his vesture and
on his thigh a name written, KING OF KINGS,
and LORD OF LORDS. (Revelation 19:6-16)

There is a lot happening here, but it is easily
understood. This answers the question of what happens
after the church is caught up. There is rejoicing and
celebration and a worship of God for salvation and His
righteous judgments. Then the attention turns to an

event that has long been awaited and that event is the marriage of the Lamb. It is when the bride of Christ (the church) is joined with her spouse (the Lord Jesus Christ) and a celebration and supper follow. It is where we become what we are to be and there will never be anything that can separate us from the Lord again.

This passage also speaks of the Lord coming back to the earth. You must grasp this concept. Until this point the Lord did not return to the earth. Everything was happening in the heavens. We were caught up to meet Him in the air and went into the marriage supper of the Lamb. Now, is the time for the Lord to come back to the earth and set up His kingdom, which means overthrowing the power that is present then. The Lord brings and army with Him who follow on white horses. So that you understand the timing of what is happening if you read on Revelation 19 you will find that this is at the time of the Battle of Armageddon. The antichrist armies are gathered and God is calling the beasts and fowls to the supper of the great God to eat of the flesh of captains, kings, and horses (vs. 17-18). This is the description of the Battle of Armageddon found in Ezekiel 38 and 39 and that is where the armies of the earth are gathered to attempt to overthrow Jerusalem and God intervenes. They meet their demise and are feasted on by the fowls and the beasts along with the creeping things of the earth.

It is at this point that the Antichrist and the False Prophet are thrown alive into the Lake of Fire and Satan will be bound for a thousand years. Joel chapter 2 describes this event well. It describes how the Lord utters His voice before His army and this great army defeats the armies of the Antichrist. That army is the church and God will lead us into battle to rescue Jerusalem from her enemies. Israel will finally see their Messiah and she will repent of her blindness. Zechariah chapters 12 through 14 give wonderful insight to the day of the Lord and in the midst of that description Zechariah let's us know of a repentance that will come over Israel and it is because they finally see their Messiah.

> *And one shall say unto him, What are these wounds in thine hands? Then he shall answer, Those with which I was wounded in the house of my friends. Awake, O sword, against my shepherd, and against the man that is my fellow, saith the Lord of hosts: smite the shepherd, and the sheep shall be scattered: and I will turn mine hand upon the little ones. And it shall come to pass, that in all the land, saith the Lord, two parts therein shall be cut off and die; but the third shall be left therein. And I will bring the third part through the fire, and will refine them as silver is refined, and will try them as gold is tried: they shall call on my name, and I will hear them: I will say, It is my people: and they shall say, The Lord is my God. (Zechariah 13:6-9)*

What a beautiful time. Messiah came as the Lamb of God to take away the sins of the world. Israel rejected her Messiah and was driven throughout the nations until 1948 when she was given back her land. Since then skirmish after skirmish have prevented her from having peace and essentially causing the turmoil we see in the world today. It will seem as though Israel is finally done but God intervenes. He rescues her and one of them will notice something strange. They will see wounds in His hands and will ask Him, what are these wounds? He will respond with those, which I was wounded in the house of my friends. They will realize that this Jesus whom they have been resisting for all this time is in fact their Messiah and a sorrowful repentance will come over them.

I am not suggesting that Israel killed the Messiah. His crucifixion was His own plan for the sin that mankind committed. Sin put Him on that cross, not Israel and not the Romans. It was our own sin, and He

113

did it because He loves us (John 15:13). Israel was the nation chosen by God to be His people and through them Messiah had to come and be rejected so that the entire world could have a chance at salvation. You might ask where in scripture do you see that? There is one place it is absolutely clear.

> *For I would not, brethren, that ye should be ignorant of this mystery, lest ye should be wise in your own conceits; that blindness in part is happened to Israel, until the fulness of the Gentiles be come in. And so all Israel shall be saved: as it is written, There shall come out of Sion the Deliverer, and shall turn away ungodliness from Jacob: For this is my covenant unto them, when I shall take away their sins. (Romans 11:25-27)*

Blindness in part happened to Israel so the Messiah could be rejected and put to death. It had to happen this way because it was Israel who God taught to sacrifice for their sin knowing that one day He, through a body that was prepared (Hebrews 10:5), would save the world of their sin and the plan of God no longer was only to Israel, but also to the gentile world. This blindness is still in effect until the fullness of the gentiles comes in and what we see in Zechariah 13 is that blindness come off and the whole house of Israel will be saved. It is a marvelous plan and one that Satan can't overthrow.

To this point we have discussed the gathering of the elect at the seventh trumpet, the marriage supper of the Lamb, the return of the Lord with His armies to the earth to destroy the enemies of Israel, and Israel's repentance upon the revelation of their Messiah. We have mentioned a thousand year reign of Christ on this earth, which is often referred to as the Millennial Reign. This describes briefly what the church will be doing after the enemies are defeated and God's wrath is poured out. Some of this passage we have seen already, but it bears repeating so we can put all this together.

> *And I saw an angel come down from heaven, having the key of the bottomless pit and a great chain in his hand. And he laid hold on the dragon, that old serpent, which is the Devil, and Satan, and bound him a thousand years, And cast him into the bottomless pit, and shut him up, and set a seal upon him, that he should deceive the nations no more, till the thousand years should be fulfilled: and after that he must be loosed a little season. And I saw thrones, and they sat upon them, and judgment was given unto them: and I saw the souls of them that were beheaded for the witness of Jesus, and for the word of God, and which had not worshipped the beast, neither his image, neither had received his mark upon their foreheads, or in their hands; and they lived and reigned with Christ a thousand years. But the rest of the dead lived not again until the thousand years were finished. This is the first resurrection. Blessed and holy is he that hath part in the first resurrection: on such the second death hath no power, but they shall be priests of God and of Christ, and shall reign with him a thousand years. And when the thousand years are expired, Satan shall be loosed out of his prison, And shall go out to deceive the nations which are in the four quarters of the earth, Gog and Magog, to gather them together to battle: the number of whom is as the sand of the sea. And they went up on the breadth of the earth, and compassed the camp of the saints about, and the beloved city: and fire came down from God out of heaven, and devoured them. And the devil that deceived them was cast into the lake of fire and brimstone, where the beast and the false prophet are, and shall be tormented day and*

night for ever and ever. And I saw a great white throne, and him that sat on it, from whose face the earth and the heaven fled away; and there was found no place for them. And I saw the dead, small and great, stand before God; and the books were opened: and another book was opened, which is the book of life: and the dead were judged out of those things which were written in the books, according to their works. And the sea gave up the dead which were in it; and death and hell delivered up the dead which were in them: and they were judged every man according to their works. And death and hell were cast into the lake of fire. This is the second death. And whosoever was not found written in the book of life was cast into the lake of fire. (Revelation 20:1-15)

This is a picture of the Millennial Reign and there is significant information to help us understand what happens when Christ returns. The devil is bound during that time. The Antichrist and False Prophet have been cast into the Lake of Fire and the Lord is now ruling as King of Kings and Lord of Lords. There is no more division on who God is and whether He exists. Scripture describes in multiple places this is a time of peace and no more suffering or sorrow. Evil's influence has been bound and God has taken away the kingdom of darkness.

During the thousand years the church shall rule with Jesus as kings and priests. This is also expressed in Revelation 1:6 and 5:9 and to those alive in the thousand years will be those who we minister to, only there will be no question who God is. After the thousand years, Satan is loosed and does what he always does and that is to deceive the nations to battle. It is at this time that Jesus Christ destroys Satan and his plan once and for all. Satan is now thrown into the Lake of Fire where the Antichrist and False Prophet are and he will never be able to deceive again.

It is at this time that God will execute the great white throne judgment to judge the dead. This is the second death. Remember, the first was resurrection unto life, the second is resurrection unto death and this is where their works judges them, since they failed to acknowledge the saving grace of God when they had the chance. Those without Jesus will be judged, contrary to the popular thinking today. Grace is now and the time to reach out to God's saving hand is now. Let Him change you now so that you can be saved while salvation is still available. Tomorrow may not come for some and to know this salvation one must believe and then repent, be baptized in Jesus name for the remission of sins, and receive the gift of the Holy Ghost (Acts 2:38).

This chapter was opened with Peter describing how the elements will melt with a fervent heat and there will be a new Heaven and a new Earth. After the great white throne judgment, God creates all things new and Revelation chapters 21 and 22 tell us of this new Heaven and new Earth. They describe a city, the New City Jerusalem who comes down from God like a bride out of Heaven and it magnificently decorated and beautifully crafted. This is the prize and from this point on we will be with Jesus forever. It is worth living for the Lord now so we can attain that eternal life and the beautiful salvation the Lord gives us. This is what it is all about and hopefully knowing this will help draw us closer to God and live His wonderful salvation that He won for us. The promise out of Revelation 22 is that He will come quickly and we know that our salvation is so much closer than the time this was written and as we discern the season, we know it is very near so we can look up for our redemption draws nigh (Luke 21:28).

He which testifieth these things saith, Surely I come quickly. Amen. Even so, come, Lord Jesus. The grace of our Lord Jesus Christ be with you all. Amen (Revelation 22:20-21)